MICHEL TREMBLAY

Michel Tremblay is a French Canadian novelist and playwright, born in Montreal, Quebec. His first professionally produced play, *Les Belles-Soeurs*, was written in 1965 and premiered at the Théâtre du Rideau Vert in August 1968. It stirred up controversy by portraying the lives of working-class women and attacking the straight-laced, deeply religious society of mid-twentieth-century Quebec. His other notable works include *À toi, pour toujours, ta Marie-Lou* (1970); *La grosse femme d'à côté est enceinte* (1978); *Albertine, en cinq temps* (*Albertine in Five Times*) (1984); *Le Vrai Monde?* (1987); and *Messe solennelle pour une pleine lune d'été* (*Solemn Mass for a Full Moon in Summer*) (1996).

DEIRDRE KINAHAN

Deirdre Kinahan is an award-winning playwright, actively involved in the Irish Theatre Sector. She is an elected member of Aosdána, Ireland's association of outstanding artists, Literary Associate with Meath Councy Council Arts Office and has served as a board member for the Abbey Theatre, Theatre Forum Ireland and the Stewart Parker Trust. Deirdre's work is translated into many languages, and produced regularly in Ireland and on the international stage.

Deirdre's other plays include *Wild Sky*, *Spinning*, *Halcyon Days*, *Moment, BOGBOY* and *Hue & Cry*. She has a series of new works in development.

Deirdre Kinahan

THE UNMANAGEABLE SISTERS

A new version of Michel Tremblay's
Les Belles-Soeurs

NICK HERN BOOKS

London

www.nickhernbooks.co.uk

A Nick Hern Book

The Unmanageable Sisters first published in Great Britain in 2018 as a paperback original by Nick Hern Books Limited, The Glasshouse, 49a Goldhawk Road, London W12 8QP, in association with the Abbey Theatre, Dublin

The Unmanageable Sisters © 2018 Deirdre Kinahan
Les Belles-Soeurs © 1968 Michel Tremblay

Deirdre Kinahan has asserted her moral right to be identified as the author of this adaptation

Front cover: Photography © Ros Kavanagh. Design © Chris Preston, Zoo Digital

Designed and typeset by Nick Hern Books, London
Printed in Great Britain by Mimeo Ltd, Huntingdon, Cambridgeshire PE29 6XX

A CIP catalogue record for this book is available from the British Library

ISBN 978 1 84842 744 0

The Unmanageable Sisters was first performed on 1 March 2018 at the Abbey Theatre, Dublin, with the following cast:

ROSE O'BRIEN	Karen Ardiff
GABBY JOYCE	Clare Barrett
LILLY DE COURCEY	Charlotte Bradley
ANGIE SMITH	Catherine Byrne
RUTHIE BARRETT	Rachael Dowling
MARIE BOYLE	Tina Kellegher
PATSY GUERIN	Lisa Lambe
JANET MOONEY	Sarah Madigan
LINDA LAWLESS	Clare Monnelly
OLIVE DOYLE	Máire Ní Ghráinne
YVONNE LONG	Mary O'Driscoll
GER LAWLESS	Marion O'Dwyer
DOLLY SNOW	Rynagh O'Grady
LISA PEARSE	Caoimhe O'Malley
TERESA DOYLE	Catherine Walsh
ADDITIONAL VOICES	Owen Roe

Director	Graham McLaren
Set Designer	Colin Richmond
Costume Designer	Joan O'Clery
Lighting Designer	Sinéad McKenna
Sound Designer	Carl Kennedy
Hair and Make-up	Val Sherlock
Voice Director	Andrea Ainsworth
Movement Coordinator	Eddie Kay
Associate Director	Sarah Baxter
Associate Dramaturg	Eleanor White
Casting	Maureen Hughes and Sarah Jones
Production Manager	Chris Hay
Stage Manager	Danny Erskine
Deputy Stage Manager	Tara Furlong
Assistant Stage Manager	Audrey Rooney
Graphic Design	Zoo Digital

6

Publicity and Production Photography	Ros Kavanagh
Sign Language Interpreter	Caroline O'Leary
Audio Description	Bríd Ní Ghruagáin and Máirín Harte
Captioning	Michael Poynor

Special thanks to Dr Lisa Goodson (NCAD) and Brian McMahon (ESB Archive).

Audio Described and Captioned performances are provided by Arts and Disability Ireland with funding from the Arts Council / An Chomhairle Ealaíon.

Abbey Theatre
Amharclann na Mainistreach

Inspired by the revolutionary ideals of our founders and our rich canon of Irish dramatic writing, our mission is to imaginatively engage with all of Irish society through the production of ambitious, courageous and new theatre in all its forms. We commit to lead in the telling of the whole Irish story, in English and in Irish, and we affirm that the Abbey is a theatre for the entire island of Ireland and for all its people. In every endeavour, we promote inclusiveness, diversity and equality.

Is é ár misean, faoi inspioráid idéil réabhlóideacha ár mbunaitheoirí agus ár gcanóin shaibhir scríbhneoireachta drámatúla de chuid na hÉireann, ná dul i dteagmháil go samhlaíoch le sochaí uile na hÉireann trí amharclannaíocht mhisniúil uaillmhianach nua de gach cineál a léiriú. Táimid tiomanta don cheannródaíocht i dtaca le scéal iomlán na hÉireann a insint, sa Bhéarla agus sa Ghaeilge, agus dearbhaímid gur amharclann í an Mhainistir d'oileán iomlán na hÉireann agus dá mhuintir uile. Déanaimid, i ngach iarracht dár gcuid, an ionchuimsitheacht, an ilchineálacht agus an comhionannas a chur chun cinn.

abbeytheatre.ie

Characters

LINDA LAWLESS
GER LAWLESS
MARIE BOYLE
GABBY JOYCE
ROSE O'BRIEN
YVONNE LONG
LILLY DE COURCEY
DOLLY SNOW
TERESA DOYLE
OLIVE DOYLE
JANET MOONEY
LISA PEARSE
ANGELA SMITH
RUTHIE BARRETT
PATSY GUERIN

This text went to press before the end of rehearsals and so may differ slightly from the play as performed.

ACT ONE

LINDA LAWLESS *enters. She sees four boxes in the middle of the kitchen.*

LINDA. Jaysus, Ma, what's all this?

GER. Is that you, Linda?

LINDA. Who owns all them boxes?

GER. They're me Green Shield Stamps.

LINDA. Your stamps! They're here already?

GER LAWLESS *enters.*

GER. Yeah, can you believe it! They arrived this mornin' just after you went to work. Wait till I tell ya, Linda, the doorbell goes and I'm in the jacks and I shout out 'Would ya hold on a minute I'm in the jacks' thinkin' it's just one of the kids off the landin' or something and then I go out and there's this hunk of a thing standin' there. Hunk! I'm telling ya, you should have seen him, Linda, you'd have fancied him, I know you would. About twenty-two he was I'd say, or twenty-three maybe, with dark curly hair and a nice little moustache and good thick arms on him. Anyway, he says to me, 'Are you Mrs Lawless?' And I said, 'Who are you, the police!?' And then he says, 'No, I have a delivery of one million stamps!' Well I nearly died I did. I nearly died. Me stamps! Me stamps was all I was thinking and I was that flabbergasted that I just kind of bleated. Just a little bleat came out. Jesus, he must of thought I was 'special' but the next thing I know two other young-fellas are haulin' in the boxes and then the handsome one is giving me this little speech. You should of heard him, he had it all practised and everything and you should have seen him, Linda. Drop-dead gorgeous he was!

LINDA. So, what did he say?

GER. What did he say?

LINDA. Yeah.

GER. I don't know what he said! I haven't a clue... something about his company and how they were real happy that I'd won a million stamps. And... and... I just couldn't say anything. I'll tell ya it's one of the only times in my life that I wished that your father was here. He would have known what to say. I don't even think I thanked the poor man and he strangled with all them boxes and he gorgeous!

LINDA. Well, it'll take you weeks to stick them all in.

GER. No it won't. There's only three boxes of stamps and the other is booklets. We'll be grand.

LINDA. We?

GER. Yes, WE! You're not going out tonight are ya?

LINDA. Of course I'm going out tonight, Ma! It's me night out with Robert...

GER. Sure you can put that eejit off, this is far more important. I rang the girls and Teresa and I went into Mrs Boyle and a few of the neighbours and they're all coming round tonight to stick in the stamps! We'll have a party. A stamp-stickin' party. It'll be a great craic! I even bought some colouredy popcorn and peanuts and sent your brother round the shops to get Coke...

LINDA. But you know I go out on a Thursday, Ma. Thursday is me Robert night. We're going to the pictures.

GER. Not tonight you're not. I've got fifteen people coming...

LINDA. Are you mad! You'll never get all them auld-ones into this kitchen! And you can't use the rest of the house coz it's in a jocker with Dad paintin' it. Jesus, Ma, sometimes I think you haven't got the brains you were born with.

GER. Oh well that's lovely that is. Put me down, why don't you. Go out and have a nice night for yourself, Linda, and I'll do everything... as per usual. I'll stick a million stamps into them books. Don't you worry about it, you just pick out all the stuff you want from the catalogue and I'll get it, I'll order it, I'll drag it up here on me back... just like I do everything...

LINDA. Jesus Christ!

GER. Jesus Christ is right!

LINDA. Would you for God's sake be reasonable...

GER. 'Reasonable... Reasonable.' Why would I want to be 'reasonable'? And all I do for you, Linda Lawless. All I do for the whole shaggin' lot of ya. Down on me knees, morning till night, scrubbin'! Scrubbin' this place and then slaving over a hot stove and I never ask for anything, do I? No, coz I wouldn't get anything, that's why and all I'm askin', all I'm askin' is that you do your bit for me with these stamps. On this the greatest night of my life, because these stamps are going to give us happiness, Linda, a new flat, new carpets, a new life! And I'm not going to stick them in them books on me own. If you want your new bedroom or your new quilt set or your new curlers then you better stay home and give me a hand right! Even your father said that if we don't get through them all this evening, he'll do a bit of sticking when he gets back from the pub.

I just wish you'd do what you're told for once instead of wasting your time on that Robert eejit.

LINDA. Robert is not an eejit!

GER. Yes he is. He's an eejit and he's a Culchie!

LINDA. Robert's from bleedin' Coolock!

GER. Exactly!... And he doesn't even make twenty pound a week! Sure the best that eejit can manage is a night out at the pictures. For Jesus' sake, Linda, you should listen to your mother and drop that waster or you'll end up without a shoe on your foot.

LINDA. Stop it, Ma. I've told you I won't be relying on Robert. I won't be relying on any man because I'm going to earn me own money!

GER. Yeah, yeah, yeah...

LINDA. And just for your information, Robert is doing very well he is. He's in training, I've told you that a thousand times and when he finishes his training he'll get more money. I've told you that. His own boss told me that. His own boss told me that Robert is a great chef and when he finishes his courses they're going to put him in charge of the whole kitchen then he'll be rolling in it!

But okay, okay I'll ring him and tell him that I can't go to the pictures. Just to keep you happy, okay! Unless… unless I ask him to come over and stick some stamps with us?

GER. Haven't I just told you that I think he's a thick and still you want to bring him over? Sometimes I wonder… I really do. What did I do to deserve such a brood? Do you know that only this morning I sent your brother out to get me twenty Major and he came back with a bottle of milk! How many times do I have to repeat meself? Repeat meself. Repeat meself! Didn't I just tell you that this party is for stickin' stamps. Didn't I just tell you that this party is women-only. Women-only. That is… women-only! So no, you can't bring Robert unless he's a poufter as well as a thick!

LINDA. Okay… Okay, Ma. Jesus. I'll tell him not to come over so. (*Muttering*.) As if I feel like stickin' stamps after workin' all day in Jacobs.

LINDA *starts to dial a number.*

And what are you doing standing there? Would ya just go and dust some of your tacky ornaments and don't be listening in to me conversation!

Hello, is Robert there? Howaya, Mrs Byrne, yeah it's Linda, I'm grand yeah. Is he there? No? Ah well will ya tell him I called? Yeah, thanks, Mrs Byrne, thanks, that's great yeah. Thanks. Yeah, I'll see ya.

She hangs up. The phone rings again straight away.

Hello?… Ma! You're wanted on the phone.

GER (*entering*). Twenty years old and you still can't say 'One moment please.'

LINDA. It's only Auntie Rose.

GER. So?

LINDA. Why would I be polite to Auntie Rose?

GER (*putting her hand over the receiver*). Shhhhhhh would ya, what if she heard you?

LINDA. I don't give a shit if she heard me!

GER (*looks at her, aghast!*). Hello? Can I ask who is this please? Oh, it's you, Rose... yes, yeah, it's me and they're here... can you believe it? A million stamps. Yeah, they're sittin' right in front of me, boxes of them. And they sent a new catalogue. And I think I'll be able to get everything! Yeah! Everything! I'll do up the whole house I will! Every room. You want to see the stuff, Rose. I'm going to get a new cooker, and a new fridge, and a new Formica table with four chairs. I fancy the red one with the gold stars embossed. I don't think you've seen that one, have ya, Rose?... Oh, it's gorgeous. And I'm gonna get new pots, new cutlery, and a non-stick frying pan, SodaStream, electric carving knife... Oh, and you know those glasses with the palm trees on them?... Well, I'm taking a set of them, too because Lilly De Courcey got a set of them last year on account of her holiday to the Canaries and she paid a fortune for them, but mine are free! She'll be bloody livid she will!... What?... Yeah, she's comin' over tonight. And they've got them fluorescent plastic tins for the flour and sugar and the coffee... so I'm getting them, I'm getting everything, everything, Rose. And one of them colonial bedroom suites with full accessories. Yeah. That's curtains, sheets and one of those things you put on the floor beside the bed... No, not a potty, Rose, Jesus!... it's called a locker or a vanity stand it says here, and new wallpaper... No not the floral, Henry won't sleep with flowers. I'm telling you, Rose, it's going to be like a hotel. And then there's the living room! Wait till you hear this... colour TV with built-in stereo, a synthetic nylon carpet, real paintings... not pictures pulled out of the calendar but you know them Chinese ones, I've had me eye on them for years, the ones with the stickin' out velvet!... Yeah. Aren't they though? Gorgeous. Wait till I tell you... crystal platters... for putting sandwiches on. Same as the ones your sister in law has but mine are nicer. And there's ashtrays... lovely brass ones in the shape of little Chinese shoes and Lava Lamps and everything. I think that's about it for the living room... but then there's an electric razor for Henry for shaving, and a shower curtains with fish on it for if you had a shower and it all comes with the stamps, Rose. I know... I know I don't have a shower but sure I'll get one put in! Or there's a sunken bath if I want it, emerald green, and a new sink with gold taps, and swimming togs for everyone... What do you mean I'm too fat? Don't you start! I've just had enough shit from Linda.... Yeah? Her room? Well... it's gonna be beautiful but yeah, okay, Rose, you can just look at the catalogue but you'll come straight over yeah? I told everyone to come early coz it's gonna take hours ya know, to stick in the stamps.

MARIE BOYLE *enters*.

Oh... Oh... here's Mrs Boyle Rose, she's just arrived, so I better go. Howaya, Marie. I'm just... I'll go now, Rose, okay love, see you in a jiff.

She hangs up.

Sorry about that, Marie.

MARIE. Are they the stamps?

GER. Yes. Yes. They are. They're the stamps.

MARIE. And that's a million is it?

GER. Yes that's a million.

MARIE. Doesn't look like a million.

GER. Well, it is a million, Marie, a million stamps...

MARIE. Some people have all the luck.

GER. Yes. Yes. They do don't they. I still can't believe it myself to be honest but can you excuse me please for a moment Marie, I'm afraid I'm not ready. I haven't got everything ready because I was just on to me sister, Rose.

MARIE. Is Rose coming over?

GER. Of course she is. Rose wouldn't miss a party for the world. So sit down why don't ya and have a look at that new catalogue. You won't believe all the stuff they have in it and I'm going to get the lot. Can you believe it, Marie, every last dish!

GER *disappears into her bedroom.*

MARIE. No I can't believe. Fat chance of me winnin' anything
like that. I'm telling ya if it was rainin' soup I'd have a fork.
Me whole life is shit and there's no sign of that changin'. A
million stamps! A whole house! I'll tell ya if I'm not careful
I might start screaming! SCREAMING! Coz it's always the
same isn't it. It's always the ones that don't deserve it get all
the luck. I mean, what did she do, Ger Lawless? Nothing,
that's what. I'm every bit as good as she is. And them
competitions should be banned in anyway, that's what Father
Scully says. He says it's gambling, gambling with God! And
they only start rows! Of course they do. Because they're not
fair, that's why. Not FAIR. I mean why should she win a
million stamps and not me? I work like a slave I do while
she sits on her arse in here in front of the telly. Two kids she
has! TWO! And I've got six! Wiping their arses I am from
morning till night and her... swanning around here like a
queen and if anything my kids are cleaner! And now I'll
have to be listening to her and her new flat and her new life.
And I'll have to listening to her blabbin' on about her
Chinese paintings and her colonial bedspread and there'll be
no end to it. Especially when I... I have to sit in me own flat
on a second-hand chair with no spring in it knowin' that
Fatso here is swamped in velvet. I'm sick of it. Sick of it all
I am. I'm sick of moppin' floors and cleanin' sinks. I'm sick
of never havin' a penny to me name. And I'm sick of me six
screamin' kids. My life is nothing. I'm nothing. And I'm fed
up of it. Fed up of this dreary rotten life.

During the monologue, GABBY JOYCE, ROSE O'BRIEN,
YVONNE LONG *and* LILLY DE COURCEY *have entered.*
They take their places in the kitchen without paying attention
to MARIE. *The five* WOMEN *get up and turn to the audience.*

THE FIVE WOMEN (*together*). This dreary, rotten life!

Monday!

LILLY. When the sun rises over the towers and starts shining on
the little daisies in the fields and the little birdies start to sing
sending their hopes up to heaven...

THE OTHER FOUR. I drag meself out of the bed and put the
batch on the grill and get out the corn flakes and boil

Bollicky his egg and then start roarin' at the rest of them to get the hell up! Then the kids eventually get out to school and Bollicky goes to work...

MARIE. Not mine, he's on the dole. He stays in bed.

THE FIVE WOMEN. Then I start on the flat. I work like a slave and I don't stop scrubbin' till noon. Then I start the washin'. Washin' dresses, washin' shirts, washin' stockings, washin' jumpers, washin' trousers, washin' tights, socks, knickers, bras. I wash it, I wring it out, I scrub it again on the stains until it's spotless and then I rinse it, I shake it, I hang it to the side. Me hands are chapped and me back is sore. And I'm cursin' this dreary rotten life and then the kids come home lookin' for their dinner and then they wreck the house and go back to school and then I hang out the clothes and then I start the tea and then they all come home and they're all knackered and they're all snarlin' at me and there's bound to be a row and then we turn on the telly.

Tuesday!

LILLY. When the sun rises over the towers...

THE OTHER FOUR. I drag meself out of the bed and put the batch on the grill. The same bloody routine. Corn flakes, tea, Bollicky's egg. I start roarin' and I shove them out the door. Then it's the ironing.

I spit, I crease, I fold and it's elbow grease till dinnertime and before I know it and the kids are in and they're starvin' and I make them jam sandwiches and I work all afternoon, polishing, airing, sweeping. Then they're all back for their tea and there's a row and then we turn on the telly.

Wednesday!...

That's the day I do me shopping. And there's no bus and I have to walk halfway into town to catch the 19A and I walk down Talbot Street and I get me meat and veg and I see all the old neighbours and I walk back down the quays and I nearly break me back with the carrier bags and I come home exhausted but I've to got to get the dinner on, and when the others come in, they're starvin' and Bollicky says I look like I've been dragged through a hedge backwards and I start shoutin' and the kids wreck the gaff and then we turn on the telly.

Thursday!

Friday!

Same routine. Same slaving. Same shouting.

Then Saturday. They're all home. Under me feet. Driving me nuts. There's bound to be a row and then we turn on the telly.

Sunday!

We go over to his mother's to watch her slaving and hear her screaming. And I have to watch the kids like a hawk so they don't break anything and I have to laugh at his auld-fella's crap jokes and eat her burnt corned beef, which everyone says is better than mine and then we go home and watch the telly.

I'm fed up with this dreary rotten life!

This dreary, rotten life! This dreary, rotten life. This dreary...

They sit down suddenly.

LILLY. On my last trip to Benidorm...

ROSE. Ah-O here we go, Benidorm!

DOLLY SNOW *gently makes her way in the door.* (*I think she might be from the country, she works hard to be one of the group, very smiley, etc.*) *Discreet little greetings are heard.*

LILLY. All I wanted to say, Rose, was that they don't do the Green Shield Stamps in Benidorm. They don't do stamps, well they do do stamps but not these ones, they only do the ones that you put on letters.

ROSE (*sarcastically*). Well, that's very interesting that is, Lilly!

The others laugh.

DOLLY. Not much fun if there's no prizes or no stamps or no catalogue. Not much fun in Benidorm.

LILLY. Oh but there is, Dolly Snow, Benidorm is beautiful, it is a destination spot.

MARIE. I've got nothing against the stamps myself, it's just the competitions I think should be banned. And that's what Father Scully said, ban the competitions, not the stamps. I mean if there were no stamps in Ireland I'd never have got me mincer.

LILLY. But why? The competitions can make families very happy.

MARIE. Yeah but they can be a pain in the arse for the people next door.

LILLY. Do you have to use that language?

MARIE. I'll say what I like, Lilly De Courcey. You're not the boss of me just because you spent a fortnight in poxy Benidorm!

ROSE. Cut it out, you two. I didn't come here to listen to fightin'. If you keep it up, I'll walk back down that stairwell and home.

GABBY. What's Ger doing in there? Is she changing or what? GER!

GER (*from the bedroom*). Just a minute. I'm having trouble getting into my... I'm having trouble with me... I can't get... Is Linda there?

GABBY. Linda? Linda! No, she's not here.

MARIE. Didn't I see her go out a while ago?

GER *comes out of her bedroom with her dress open at the back.*

GER. Didn't you what, Marie?

Don't tell me that little cow has snuck out?

GABBY. Can we start sticking these stamps then Ger, while we're waiting for ya?

GER. No! I've got to tell you what to do. I won't be a minute. I'll get another dress. Don't do anything till I get out there. Just... chat among yourselves like.

GABBY. 'Chat among ourselves'? What the fuck does that mean?

The telephone rings.

ROSE. Hello… Linda? No, she's not here, she's gone out actually… but if you want to wait I think she'll be back soon…

She puts the receiver down, goes out on the balcony and shouts.

Linda! Linda, you're wanted.

LILLY. So, how's Ciara getting on since the wedding, Mrs Long?

YVONNE. Oh, she's as happy as Larry thank you, Mrs De Courcey. Having a great life. She was telling me all about her honeymoon!

ROSE. Oh yeah!

GABBY. Where did they go to, Mrs Long?

YVONNE. The Canary Islands

GABBY/ROSE/DOLLY. Wooo, fancy…

YVONNE. You see her Patrick won the holiday in a competition in work which was marvellous but it meant we had to bring the wedding forward a few months.

ROSE. Six months wasn't it, Mrs Long.

GABBY. Rose!

ROSE. Sure there's nothing new to that wan, only the cutting of the cake.

DOLLY. Whereabouts are the Canary Islands, Mrs Long?

LILLY. Off the coast of Africa, Dolly. We holidayed there once. It's an archipelago…

ROSE. Arc-your-what?!

Everyone laughs.

LILLY. Beautiful islands, Dolly… but the women there like to sunbathe topless.

ROSE. Jesus! Topless! Are ya serious? My Des would love that…

LILLY. And I wouldn't call the Canary natives very clean. They don't wash regularly.

DOLLY. Really? Like the eyeties living next door to me. You wouldn't believe the hum off them!

LILLY. Did you ever notice that Italian woman's clothesline of a Monday?

DOLLY. No, why?

LILLY. No underwear!

MARIE. You're kidding!

ROSE. No knickers?

LILLY. I don't think they wear any.

YVONNE. You're joking!

LILLY. God's truth! Take a look for yourself next Monday.

DOLLY. Their trousers must be rotten!

MARIE. Or maybe the mother is just shy and hangs them up in her kitchen?!

The others laugh.

LILLY. Italians! Shy? Are you mad, Marie! Them Mediterraneans are mad for it! Sure you only have to look at their films – Pornographic is what they are… you wouldn't see the likes of it here in Ireland. Sure they stand right out in the middle of the street and kiss, in broad daylight… tongues and everything! But they can't help it I believe. It's in their blood. Just take a look at the Italian daughter when she brings her boyfriend round! It's a shocking disgrace is what it is. A shocking disgrace.

Which reminds me, Rose. I think I saw your Michael with her the other day…

ROSE. My Michael? Not with that slut…?

LILLY. I'm afraid so.

ROSE. You must be mistaken, Mrs De Courcey. It couldn't have been my Michael.

LILLY. They must have thought no one could see them. They were all over each other on the front balcony…

DOLLY. That's true, Rose. I saw them too. Kissing the face off each other… and kind of squirming like!

ROSE. The little bastard! I'll kill him. As if one randy get isn't enough in the family. His father's the same, can't even see a bikini on the telly without getting a stiffy. What is it with men? It's not natural. Sex. Sex. Sex. It's all my lot think about.

GABBY. Well, Jesus, Rose, you don't have to broadcast it to the whole nation!

LILLY. Though we're very interested…

DOLLY *and* MARIE. Yes, we are…

YVONNE. But to get back to Ciara's honeymoon…

GER (*entering*). Here I am, girls!

Greetings, 'how are you's', etc.

So, what have you all been chatting about?

ROSE. Sex and Ciara Long's honeymoon.

GER. Oh really!? (*To* YVONNE.) Well, that's nice. Hello, Yvonne…

(*To* ROSE.) And what was it Yvonne was saying?

ROSE. Oh it sounds like they had a great trip altogether. Met all sorts of people and went on a boat didn't they, Yvonne. A big boat. Then they went visiting islands, of course, the Canary Islands… so they went fishing I suppose and they caught a few canaries… sure what else?! And huge colourful fish no doubt and then they ran into some couples that they knew and had a sing-song. And then they all came home on the same flight and lived happily ever after.

YVONNE. Well…

ROSE. Amn't I right, Yvonne, isn't that what happened isn't it?

YVONNE. As a matter of fact…

GER. Well, you tell Ciara that I wish her all the best. We all do. Even though none of us was invited to her big fancy wedding.

There is an embarrassed silence.

GABBY. Is that the Angelus I hear?

GER. Is it six o'clock? Jesus! I'll just get me beads.

She goes out.

ROSE. What does she want with Rosary beads after winning all that?

DOLLY. Maybe she's having trouble with her kids…?

GABBY. No, she would have told me…

GER (*from the bedroom*). Goddamn it! Where's me beads?

ROSE. I don't know, Gabby. Our sister likes to keep things to herself.

GABBY. Not with me she doesn't. She tells me everything. You're the one can't be trusted, you're the one with the big mouth.

ROSE. Jesus! Did you hear that?

GABBY. Sure everyone knows you can keep nothing to yourself.

ROSE. Isn't that lovely…

LILLY. Please, ladies! Wasn't it you, Rose O'Brien, who just said that you didn't come here to listen to quarrelling?

ROSE. Ah shut the hell up, Lilly De Courcey. I didn't say quarrelling… who says 'quarrelling'?… I said 'fight'!

GER *comes back in with her Rosary beads.*

GER. What's going on? I can hear you roarin' at the other end of the flat!

GABBY. Nothing, it's just Rose.

GER. Well, settle down, Rose. You're supposed to be the life and soul of the party…

No fighting tonight!

ROSE. See! In any normal family you say 'fight' not stupid-arse 'quarrelling'.

GER now starts the Rosary. All the WOMEN *get down on their knees with varying levels of enthusiasm. After a few 'Hail Marys', a great racket is heard outside. The* WOMEN *scream and run to the door.*

GER. Oh my God! Me sister-in-law Teresa's mother-in-law just fell down three flights of stairs!

ROSE. Did you hurt yourself, Mrs Doyle?

GABBY. She's probably dead!

TERESA (*from a distance*). Are you all right, Mother? (*A faint moan is heard.*) Wait a minute. Let me get that wheelchair off of you. Is that better? Now I'm going to try help you back into your chair. You need to work with me, Mother. Make an effort. Don't just let yourself slide like that. Ouch! Stop it would you, Mother.

DOLLY. Here, Mrs Doyle. Can I give you a hand?

TERESA. Yes, thank you, Dolly. You are so kind.

The other WOMEN *come back into the room.* ROSE *wheels in the wheelchair.*

ROSE. Jesus, I'm a nervous wreck after all that!

GER. What about my novena?

ROSE. Sure pick it up tomorrow and you'll be finished by Saturday.

DOLLY *now enters with* TERESA DOYLE. DOLLY *has* OLIVE DOYLE *flung over her shoulder.*

GER. Jesus help us, is she hurt bad?

TERESA. No, she's well used to it. She falls out of that chair about ten times a day with the shakin'.

God help us I'm pantin'. It's no joke, hauling that thing up them stairs. Do you have anything to drink for me, Ger?

GER. Of course… Gabby, get Teresa a glass of water.

TERESA. Water!?

GER *approaches* OLIVE, *still hanging on* DOLLY's *back.*

GER. And how are you today, Mrs Doyle?

TERESA. Don't get too close, Ger. She's started biting lately.

In fact, OLIVE *tries to bite* GER's *hand.*

GER. Jesus, she's dangerous! How long has she been doing that?

TERESA. Honestly, you've no idea what I have to put up with,
I'm at the end of my rope! You can't imagine life stuck with
your mother-in-law and it's not that I don't love her, the poor
woman, but she's deranged at this stage, I can't take my eyes
off her or she's destroyed the place.

DOLLY. Do you think I can put her down now?

No one pays any attention; they are all focused on TERESA.

ROSE. How come she's not in hospital, Teresa?

TERESA. Because when Barny got a raise, the Social stopped
paying for her care. If we left her in the hospital we would
have had to pay all the bills ourselves!

MARIE. Is that a fact?!

YVONNE. That's shockin'!

DOLLY. I'll just pop her back into her chair so, will I?

No one answers so DOLLY *sits* OLIVE *into her chair and
tries to settle her.*

During TERESA's *speech,* GER *opens the boxes and
distributes the stamps and books.*

TERESA. We had to bring her home. No choice, and the woman
is ninety-three years old. It's like having a baby again in the
house. I have to dress her, undress her, wash her…

DOLLY. God help us, poor Mrs Doyle…

YVONNE. You poor thing, Teresa.

TERESA. You've no idea! Only this morning, I said to our
Paddy… 'Mammy's going shopping, so you stay here and
mind your granny.' Well, when I got home hadn't the old bat

dumped a jar of honey all over herself and was playing in it like a toddler. Of course, Paddy had scarpered and I had to clean the table, the floor, the wheelchair...

DOLLY. And what about Mrs Doyle?

TERESA. Well, I left her in it, obviously. If she's going act like a baby, I'll have to treat her like a baby, Dolly. To teach her a lesson.

GER. You'll get your reward in heaven, Teresa Doyle.

DOLLY. You will. You're too good to her so you are.

GABBY. Absolutely... too good.

TERESA. We all have our crosses to bear. I just tell myself that God is good and he's going to help me get through this.

LILLY. You'll have me crying in a minute!

TERESA. Oh no, Mrs De Courcey, don't go upsetting yourself over me!

DOLLY. I think you're a real saint.

GER. Well, now that's marvellous, Teresa. So you've all got your stamps and your booklets, I'll put a little water in some saucers and we can get started, yeah? We don't want to spend the whole night just blabbin', do we?!

She fills a few saucers and passes them around. The WOMEN *start pasting stamps in the books.* GER *goes out on the balcony.*

If Linda's out there, she can come in and give us a hand? Ricko, have you seen Linda? She's what? Down The Penter? I don't believe it! Down the pub and me here waitin' on her. Be an angel, Ricko, will ya, and go down and tell her to get home immediately. Then come see me in the morning and I'll give you a bag of popcorn if there's any left. Okay, love? Good man!

She comes back inside.

Can you believe that? And the little bitch promised to stay home.

MARIE. Kids are all the same.

TERESA. You can say that again!

GABBY. No respect! Sure I'm driven mad by our Raymond since he started that music programme for the gifted down at the Holy Spirit School. Unbearable he is, I'm telling you, you wouldn't know him! He goes around the flat humming Mozart. Mozart! for fuck's sake, and with his nose in the air an' all. And now he's taken to answering me back in Latin! Latin! And then he starts playing that violin they gave him… Jesus, it's like a bag of drownin' cats and then he wants to watch these music programmes on the telly… BBC2 if you don't mind and sometimes in the middle of the afternoon! And if there's one thing I can't stand it's that classical music… all that bangin'!

ROSE. Yeah, it's not good for them is it? Too much education.

Didn't the bishops warn us!

Too much education will give the kids notions.

TERESA. And then when the flutes come in, screeching like. I always think that classical music would blow your head off!

GABBY. Of course, Raymond says we just don't understand it. We're not ourtistic! As if he's better than us. Better than his own mother and father! Well I didn't send him to that special class so he could look down on us, I've a good mind to pull him out and get him a job with the maintenance like his brother.

ALL. They give ya no thanks, kids. They give ya no thanks.

GER. Be sure to keep filling in those books won't ya, girls? Stamps on every page.

ROSE. Would ya relax, Ger, you'd think we'd never seen a Green Shield Stamp before!

YVONNE. Isn't it getting roastin' in here? Can we open a winda…

GER. No. It might cause a draught and I'd be afraid for me stamps!

ROSE. They're not birds are they? They're not going to fly away, Ger! Not like Bernie's missus, did I ever tell you about

Bernie's missus... Gaga she is... daft as fuck, you remember Bernie? Me eldest? He was a good boy, Bernie, he never should have married that crazy. You had want to see the state of their house.

Spotlight on ROSE.

You see last Easter Bernie went and picked up a birdcage for the two kids with two little birds and all in it. And the minute he brought it home didn't Gaga go gaga over it. And two birdies wasn't enough for her, no! So now she's got eight birdies and she lets them out and all she does, so they can stretch their little wings and they shitting all over the place and then she sends the kids runnin' round trying to catch them saying, 'Catch Mammy's little birdies, catch Mammy's little birdies.' I'm telling you, it's a madhouse.

And Bernie humours her no end, that's what I can't understand, hugs her and all he does, in front of his own mother, sayin', 'Isn't she great, isn't she so soft-hearted'... 'Soft in the bleedin' head,' is what I want to say.

The WOMEN *are in stitches.*

And then there's the kids! She has no control over them, none! Lets them do what they like, I'll tell you the young ones nowadays have no idea how to discipline their kids.

GER. You said it, Rose.

MARIE. Never a truer word.

ROSE. I mean, who lets children play in the toilet? Who? You should have seen it last Sunday. The two of them just head into the jacks after the Sunday dinner, like it is the normal thing like and then they start to turn on the water! Rolling themselves in the toilet roll they were and makin' little boats out of it and Gaga says, 'Aren't they so creative at that age,' and I... I sitting up to me ankles in water...well, I snapped I did, I couldn't take another minute of their enjoyin' theirselves so I gave Bruno (I mean who the fuck calls their kid Bruno) a good clip around the ear for himself and I ate the pair of them and sent them off to bed.

GABBY. Exactly what they needed, Rose!

ROSE. And then of course Gaga starts crying. Says she won't have me terrorising her children. And Bernie sticks up for her... my Bernie... and kisses her and everything and tells her not to be worrying so I told him straight I did. 'We'll have less of your happy families thank you very much,' I said, 'you need to put some manners on that one or you'll be a laughing stock... we'll all be a laughing stock... because she cares more about them birds,' I said, 'than she does her own kids.'

'She'll sprout wings next!' I said and with a bit of luck might throw herself out the bloody window!

They all laugh.

YVONNE. Oh you're a riot, Rose.

GABBY. Yeah, never a dull moment...

ROSE. Yeah... Yeah, sure you have to laugh, don't you? Every story has a silver lining...

TERESA. Not every story...

DOLLY. No. It must be very hard for you, Teresa, with all you have to put up with.

Yet you're always thinking of other people.

ROSE. What you need to do is put yourself first sometimes, Teresa. Get yourself a night out.

TERESA. A night out! A night out! Who would look after Mrs Doyle? Not to mention the other problem...

GER. Don't tell us there's more!

TERESA. You've no idea, girls! You see now that Barny, my husband is doing very well and making more money like the whole family think we're millionaires. And they're all arriving to the door with their hands out!

GER. No!

TERESA. Only yesterday, a sister-in-law of my sister-in-law comes to the house with her own tale of woe. Now, her situation is a real heartbreaker so I gave her a bag of old clothes and stained sheets and she was that grateful that she wanted to kiss my hand!

DOLLY. No?!… Like the Pope!

MARIE. No more than you deserve, Teresa.

TERESA. I suppose we all do our best.

DOLLY. An absolute saint!

LILLY. We will include you in our prayers, Teresa.

TERESA. Well, I always say that 'If God put poor people on this earth, they ought to be encouraged.'

GER. Marvellous! Now when you're all finished filling a book, instead of piling them on the table, why don't we put them back in the box? Give us a hand, Rose, we'll take out the empty books and put the full ones back in.

ROSE. Right so. Dear God! Would ya look at all these? We'll never get though them all them tonight.

GER. We will of course, anyways, not everyone's here yet…

DOLLY. Oh who else is coming, Mrs Lawless?

GER. Ruthie Barrett and Angela Smith. They're comin' over after a funeral mass. One of their old Maggie-friends has a daughter whose husband keeled over. His name was Fagan I think.

YVONNE. Not Rory Fagan?…

GER. Yeah, I think so…

YVONNE. I used to do a line with him! Imagine, if I'd married him I'd be a widow today!

GABBY. Guess what, girls? I got the eight mistakes in that spot-the-mistake competition in the paper last Sunday. I've been tryin' to spot them for months, so I sent the answer in…

YVONNE. And did you win anything?

GABBY. Do I look like someone that's ever won anything?

TERESA. What are you going to do with all these stamps, Ger?

GER. Didn't I tell you? I'm going to do up the whole flat. Hang on and I'll show you the catalogue. Wait till you see all the stuff I'm gonna get for nothin'!

TERESA. For nothing! You mean it's not going to cost you a penny?

GER. No, not a penny. Aren't these competitions just brilliant?

LILLY. Marie doesn't think so.

GER. Marie doesn't?

MARIE. I didn't say anything!

ROSE. Yes you did. You said that these competitions are not fair because only one family wins.

MARIE. Well, that's true isn't it. Lotteries and competitions are a racket. I'm against them.

GER. That's just because you never won anything.

MARIE. They're not fair.

GER. Did ya ever hear the like! You're just jealous, Marie Boyle, and I'll tell you something, I don't like jealousy and I don't like jealous people. In fact jealous people really piss me off.

MARIE. Oh do they now! Grand, you can stick your soggy stamps up your arse!

LILLY. Mother of God, Marie…

MAIRE *makes as if to leave.*

GER. Ah no, don't go… don't be going home for God's sake. I'm sorry I am, I'm sorry, sure me nerves is gone from all this, I don't know what I'm saying. Let's just forget it and keep on stickin', here, Marie, have a few peanuts for yourself.

ROSE. Our sister is afraid of losing one of her skivvies!…

GABBY. Why don't you mind your own business, Rose.

MARIE. All right, I'll stay. But I don't think them competitions are fair and that's final.

From this point on, MARIE will steal all the books she fills. The others will see what she's doing right from the start, except for GER, obviously, and they will decide to follow suit.

LILLY. Well, I figured out the puzzle in one of last month's *Woman's Weekly*s.

DOLLY. Did you, Lilly?

LILLY. It was easy enough… The first clue was a Persian king…

ROSE. Onassis was it?

LILLY. No, a Persian king… That's a 'shah'.

YVONNE. A shag is a Persian? I thought a shag was a rug.

ROSE. I thought it was a ride!

They all laugh.

LILLY. I said shah, Yvonne. A shah is a Persian king.

And the second clue, is something that the Vikings did.

ROSE. Ride?

They all laugh again.

LILLY. Raid. Viking used to *raid* towns.

So the whole answer is a game you play at parties.

ROSE. Spin the Bottle!

GABBY. Rose, will you shut up for God's sake!

(*To* LILLY.) Scrabble?

LILLY. No! It's easy. Shah and raid… Charade!

DOLLY. What's a charade?

LILLY. I figured it out in no time.

YVONNE. So, did you win anything?

LILLY. Do I look like I need to win anything! I didn't bother to send it in. I just did it for the challenge.

DOLLY. You're very clever, Mrs De Coursy.

ROSE. I love them competitions in the magazines, especially the word ones. Mystery words, hidden words, crosswords, turned-around words, all that stuff with words. It's me specialty. I've broken all records for enterin'. I never miss a contest… costs me about a pound a week just for stamps.

YVONNE. So, do you win anything?

ROSE (*looking at* GER). Do I look like someone that's ever won anything?

TERESA. Mother! Will you let go of my saucer?... Jesus, would ya look what she's done. Gone and spilt it all over herself! She has me heart broke...

She hits OLIVE *on the head and the latter settles down a little.*

GABBY. Dear God, you don't take any jip from her do ya? Aren't you afraid ya might hurt her?

TERESA. Not at all, she's well used to it. My husband figured it out, if you give her a good belt, it kind of paralyses her and then she calms down in an instant.

YVONNE. And that's medical advice is it?

TERESA. Oh yes, it is, it's medical!

Blackout.

Spotlight on YVONNE.

YVONNE. I can't tell you how proud I am of Ciara. She's a great girl she is and when she got back from her honeymoon, didn't she give me the top part of her wedding cake, as a thank-you like! And it is so lovely it is. A little church at the top of it, all made of icing and it's got red-velvet stairs leading up to a kind of a platform and on the top of the platform stand this little bride and groom. Two little dolls all dressed up like they're getting married. There's even a little priest-fella to bless them and behind him there's an altar and it's all icing. I never knew you could do that, I've never seen anything so... perfect. Of course, it cost a fortune. The cake. Six levels on it. It wasn't all cake though. Sure who could afford that? Just the first two levels were cake. The rest of it was wood. But isn't it incredible what people can do. You'd never have known it wasn't all cake. Anyway, Ciara gave me the top part and she had it set like under this special glass bell and I was, well I was very weepy because it looked so... perfect with the three little figurines... like a play, I like a play, I go to the amateur plays in the parish hall and I like them because I think a play is like a dream... a dream from the everyday but it's free, that's the difference, you can change it... change the ending, move those little figurines any way you like and make it perfect but then I was afraid that it might spoil, the cake… you know, without air. So I took my husband's glass knife… He's got a special knife for cutting glass… And I cut a hole in the top of the bell so that the air can get in and now the icing won't go bad and she'll have a good life, Ciara, I want her to have a good life, a better life…

DOLLY. I had a go at a contest once. It was in the *Ireland's Own*. You had to come up with a slogan for a new bookshop in Wexford called Hachettes. I spent hours at it and I came up with… 'Hachette's will chop the cost of your books.'

ROSE. Yeah?

DOLLY. Hachette. Hatchet and chop like.

YVONNE. Oh yes, very good, Dolly, but did you win anything?

DOLLY. Do I look like someone that's ever won anything?

GER. I saw your Brendan out cutting the grass, Yvonne, with a clippers. You should buy yourself a lawnmower. I'd be afraid he'd have a heart attack with that belly on him. I'll be getting a lawnmower with me stamps…

DOLLY. Her and her stamps, she's starting to get on my nerves.

She hides a booklet in her purse.

ROSE. What are you gonna do with a lawnmower on the ninth floor?

GER. You never know, it might come in handy. And who knows, we might get a nice little house like Lilly someday.

MARIE. Next she'll tell us she needs a bigger flat for all her stuff!

GER. You know, when I think of it, we'll probably need to get a bigger flat for all our stuff!

DOLLY, MARIE and TERESA all hide two or three books each.

TERESA. Do you ever listen to the mystery voice on the radio? Well, I guessed it last week. It was that politician Noël Browne, it was me husband figured it out coz the clue was 'He's always getting fired.' So I sent in the entry twenty-five times just to be sure that they'd get it. I even signed it from my youngest... for luck like.

YVONNE. Did you win anything?

TERESA (*looking to* GER). Do I look like someone that's ever won anything?

GABBY. Do you know what my husband's talking about getting me for my birthday?

ROSE. Two pairs of nylons, same as last year!

GABBY. No! A fur coat! Not real fur mind but I don't care coz I think the synthetics are gorgeous. You'd want to be off your rocker to pay what they pay for the real fur!

LILLY. I'm afraid I can't agree with you there, Gabby...

ROSE. Here we go...

LILLY. I just think it's important to point out, Rose, that the real thing is the real thing. That synthetic is nothing like fur. In fact, I'll be updating my stole for the new season. The old one is starting to look a bit ratty... it's mink but that's the problem with mink...

ROSE. Of course it is. Didn't I just say that to my Des this evening, don't be buying me mink, Des, it gets fierce ratty it does! Sure we all know your husband's down the pawn shop most weeks, Lilly De Courcey, because he's up to his neck in debt with you and your mink stoles...

LILLY. If your husband wants to buy my stole, Gabby, you can tell him I'll sell it to him cheap. Then you'll have something real.

ROSE. What a Christian heart you have, Lilly!

YVONNE. Personally I like that inflated objects game in the RTÉ Guide, the one where you guess what the object is. Last week I guessed a screw, a screwdriver and some kind of bent-up hook.

THE OTHERS. So...?

DOLLY. I heard a good joke the other day...

ROSE. Did ya? So tell us, Dolly!

DOLLY. Oh, I couldn't. I'm no good at telling jokes and besides it's a bit rude.

ROSE. Ah go on, Dolly, we know you've got a stack of them!

DOLLY. No. I'm too embarrassed. I don't know why, but I am...

GABBY. Don't be such a tease, Dolly Snow, tell us your joke!

DOLLY. Okay... All right... There was a young teacher down in the national school...

ROSE. Good start...

DOLLY. She's after reading the story of Robin Hood to the kids and she was askin' them questions to see what they learnt and she says, 'Who was Robin Hood's girlfriend?'

And this young fella says, 'Trudy.' She says 'No. It was Marion. Maid Marion.'

And he says, 'Oh yeah, and what about the song? "Robin Hood, Robin Hood, riding Trudy Glenn".'

All the WOMEN *burst out laughing.*

ROSE. Ah Jaysus, that's a good one, Dolly. Where did ya get it from?

GABBY. You know where she got it from, Rose, from her secret admirer, that little fella sells the toilet brushes!

DOLLY. Don't say that...!

ROSE. Oooh... tell us more, Dolly!

LILLY. I don't understand.

GABBY. There's a little pedlar comes to the flats of a Thursday and I think Dolly's got her eye on him!

DOLLY. Please, Gabby....

ROSE. One thing's for sure, Dolly's toilet is spotless! I saw him only yesterday heading into The Penter. He must have been paying a visit was he, Dolly?

DOLLY. Well, he called all right...

All the WOMEN *go 'WOOO-OOO'.*

...but there's nothing going on. I promise.

ROSE. Like we haven't heard that before!

DOLLY. Please, Rose, don't go twisting everything. Mr Simon is a good man he is.

ROSE. I'm sure he is! But who's to say that you're a good girl, Dolly!

DOLLY. Rose!

ROSE. Ah now don't go gettin' all het up, I'm only slagging ya!

DOLLY. Then please don't be saying things like that. Of course, I'm good. And I'm respectable and I go to confession every Saturday and the only reason Bar– I mean Mr Simon called was because he wants me to hostess one of those Home-Ware parties where he can give us a demo...

ROSE. Oooooh, a demo is it!

DOLLY. A demonstration of his bathroom gadgets.

They all laugh uproariously

ROSE. Is that bathroom or bedroom, Dolly?!

DOLLY. I don't know what you're all laughing at, he only asked me because he knows my flat and if I get ten people I get a free gift so I said I would and it's next Sunday after eleven o'clock mass. And the gift is only gorgeous so it is, it's four of them china cups with pictures of the city of Limerick on them. Mr Simon brought them back from his holidays. They must have cost him a fortune. So would yiz come do you think?

ROSE. Will you come? That's the question, Dolly...

They all laugh again.

DOLLY. Stop. Please. Will you stop.

ROSE. Oh all right then but you're a scream, Dolly Snow.

So are there any door prizes?

DOLLY. I don't know. I'll ask Mr Simon but I'll definitely be making tea and sandwiches.

ROSE. That's more than you get around here! We'll be lucky if we see a glass of juice at this stage!...

OLIVE *starts to sing some old Dirty Dublin song – maybe 'Dicey Reilly'.*

Jaysus, what's kicked her off!

TERESA. That used to be her party piece. I must of said that we were going to a party. Stop it, Mother, or I'll throw you over the balcony.

ROSE. Some party… not even a nip of gin!

Blackout. Spotlight on DOLLY.

DOLLY. I wish they wouldn't laugh at me like that. Mr Simon doesn't laugh at me. Mr Simon likes to hear me laugh. The first time I saw him I'll admit I thought that he was as ugly as sin. He's not good looking in the usual way so when he called to the flat one Thursday and said, 'Would you like to take a look at my brushes?' I slammed the door in his face. My mother always told me never to let a man in the flat! I think that might have been what happened to her back in Wexford so the only one who gets into my flat is the paperboy because he's still too young to get any ideas. Well, about a month later didn't Mr Simon call back and he was all red in the face because it was a hot day and the lift was broke and he was puffing and panting so I let him come into the hallway and sit down in the cool of it. But then when he was inside, I got a bit scared but then I thought I'm bigger than he is and he's bald and he wears very nice clothes so maybe he isn't dangerous. And actually, he turned out not to be a bit dangerous but quite a gentleman, not that I've ever met too many gentlemen but he was, is, nice, and very polite. So I bought two toilet brushes from him on that first day and then he took out his catalogue and there were lovely things in it for the bathroom. And I fancied this little peach soapholder with a white flower on it but he didn't have one with him so he said I could place an order. Me! Dolly Snow, placing an order! I felt very important. Ever since then, he calls back to me once a fortnight and sometimes I don't buy things but we just have a cup of tea and a chat. And when he's talking you kind of forget that he's ugly because he knows things. He travels all around Dublin and out to Meath and Wicklow and he's even been to Wexford where I was born and lived the first ten years of me life and he says

Wexford is a grand county and I... I think I'm in love with him... I know that might sound stupid because I only see him for that hour, once a fortnight but I look forward to his visits and I buy them fondant fancies from Mary's shop on the Sillogue Road to go with the tea and he loves the pink icing on them and he licks his lips if a little bit of the sugary bit escapes and I've never felt this way before. Never. I mean men have never paid me too much attention. I've never actually had a boyfriend because I was always busy with work in the hospital and minding Mammy but he tells me all about his travels and the kind of people he meets so one day I bought a bit of lipstick in the chemist and put it on and now sometimes he tells me jokes or rude stories and at first I was scarlet to be honest, but sometimes they're very funny and he says he loves the way I laugh so I laugh, I laugh and laugh and laugh for him. And it's only lately that they got a bit extra spicy and sometimes that makes me feel uncomfortable but then the other day he brushed against my hand and I went pink I did, so then he held my hand and my stomach started turning inside out and I thought I'd die because his little hand was in my big hand and he stroked my arm. Jesus! I suddenly felt roasting all over and I didn't want him to ever leave the flat. OR ever take his hand away because I love him coming around and I haven't held anyone's hand since Mammy died and I dream about him now every night and I dream that we're married and we're living all happy in my flat and the place is shining with all his tea cups and brushes and he's the first man who ever cared about me and I don't want to lose him. I don't want Mr Simon to go away and I'm kind of terrified now on a Thursday that he won't come because then I'll be all on my own again and how would I ever meet anyone? I need someone... I just want someone to love.

The lights come on again. LINDA *and her two friends* JANET MOONEY *and* LISA PEARSE *enter.*

GER. Well, would you look what the cat's dragged in.

LINDA. I was only down at The Penter.

GER. I know you were down at The Penter and if you keep hanging around bars you're going to end up like your Auntie Pats down on Fitzwilliam Square!

LINDA. Give me a break will you.

GER. I asked you to stay home…

LINDA. I only went down to get a packet of fags and then I met
Janet and Lisa!

GER. That's no excuse. You knew I was havin' the girls over
and you knew I needed you to help me and that's why you
didn't come back from your precious Penter, isn't it. Honest
to God you pull the heart out of me, Linda Lawless, and you
do it on purpose. You just want to make a show of me in
front of my friends. Just wait till I tell your father!

ROSE. Don't be giving her a hard time, Ger.

GABBY. I'd stay out of it if I were you, Rose.

LINDA. So, I'm a little late! Jesus Christ, it's not the end of
the world!

LISA. It's our fault, Mrs Lawless.

JANET. Yeah, it's our fault, we bought her a drink…

GER. I know it's your fault. And I've told Linda a thousand
times not to be hanging around with tramps. But she doesn't
listen to anyone.

ROSE. For God's sake, Ger…

GABBY. Honestly, Rose, you need to mind your own business…

ROSE. Would ya shut up you, Gabby. Me niece is getting the
head chewed off in front of the whole block and for no good
reason!

GABBY. So? It's got nothing to do with you!

LINDA. Leave her alone, Auntie Gabby. She's only defending
me…

GABBY. But that's my job. I'm your godmother!

GER. You see what I have to put up with!

ROSE. Well, you're the one that reared her!

GER. How dare you! Like your pack are any better…

LINDA. Go on, Auntie Rose, give it to her between the eyes!

GER. So, it's Auntie Rose is it. 'Auntie Rose' this, 'Auntie Rose' that. Have you forgotten what you said when she was on the phone earlier?

LINDA. That was different.

ROSE. Why, what did she say?

GER. Well, when she answered the phone to you earlier, I was giving out because she was too ignorant to say, 'One moment, please,' like I'm always tellin' her to. So I said you should to be more polite to your Auntie Rose...

LINDA. Will ya shut up, Ma...

ROSE. No don't shut up, Ger. I want to know what she said...

LINDA. But it's not important, it was her that was doing me head in!

GER. So she said, 'It's only Aunt Rose. Why should I be fucking polite to her?'

ROSE. I don't believe it...

LINDA. She's twistin' it!

ROSE. I never would have thought that of you, Linda.

GABBY. Well, I told you to stay out of it.

ROSE. I've never been so insulted. And all I do for you, Linda Lawless. Your mother's right, if you're not careful you'll end up whoring around the place like your Auntie Pats, I've a good mind to give you a slap.

GER. Just you try it! No one lays a hand on my kids but me!

TERESA. Dear God, will you give it a rest... it's like the Ballymun Boxing Club in here.

DOLLY. We're exhausted listening to you.

TERESA. And if you wake up Mother, she'll start biting again.

GER. So?! She's your problem. I don't know what you're doing bringing her round here in anyways!

TERESA. Well, isn't that lovely...

GABBY. Ger's right, it's not natural to be bringing that auld geriatric with you to parties.

LILLY. I thought I just heard *you* telling *Rose* to mind her own business?

GABBY. Keep your own nose out of it, you stuck-up bitch…

LILLY *gets up*.

LILLY. How dare you!

OLIVE *spills the saucer she has been playing with*.

TERESA. Ah now would you look what you made her do!

GER. Me good tablecloth!

ROSE. She's soaked me, the old bag!

TERESA. That's not true! You weren't even close!

ROSE. Are you calling me a liar!

TERESA. Yes, you are a liar!

GER. Jesus, she's fallen out of her chair!

DOLLY. Oh, no, she's on the floor, again!

TERESA. Somebody give me a hand.

ROSE. Not a chance!

GABBY. Pick her up yourself.

DOLLY. Here, Mrs Doyle, I'll help you.

TERESA. Thank you, Dolly, at least there's one 'lady' in the place.

GER (*to* LINDA). And you watch your step, young lady. See what you started and we all having such a lovely friendly evening.

LINDA. I'm going back to the pub.

GER. Well, if you do I'm locking that door and you can go and live on the streets!

LINDA. Like I haven't heard that before!

TERESA. For God's sake, Mother. Just sit still and I'll try strap you in.

MARIE. I'll hold the chair.

TERESA. Thank you, Marie…

ROSE. If it was me, I'd take that chair and wrap it around her neck…

GABBY. Rose, don't start again!

TERESA. As if I haven't enough problems…

GABBY. Would ya get a load of Lilly De Courcey still sitting there like an angel lickin' her stamps. As if all this wasn't happening. Lilly De Courcey, bet you think you're so much better than us don't ya…

Blackout.

Spotlight on LILLY DE COURCEY.

LILLY. I don't think. I know, Gabby Guerin. Honest to God it's like visiting Dublin Zoo. Leo was right, he told me not to come tonight. I should have stayed home. We don't belong here any more, we're well off out of it. Once you've tasted life in Glasnevin, you should never come back. I can just picture myself now in my polished living room, watching *Songs of Praise* on the telly or walking in my own front door, through the rose garden, a library book under my arm and the postman looking at me like I'm something. I think he was actually giving me the eye yesterday, that postman. Maybe I should have passed the time of day with him, he seemed nice, country. It's hard to get a word out of most of the neighbours in Glasnevin. They keep themselves to themselves, not like this crowd, ignorant, gossips, every one of them. You see they don't travel, that's their problem. They don't get any further than Inchicore! You'd never meet a GER LAWLESS in Benidorm. Never! Only people of quality and ambition go to Spain. This lot would drag you down to the gutter and keep you there. I'll never set foot in these blessed flats again. I shouldn't have come. I shouldn't talk to the Guerins, they behave like fishwives. Honest to God, I'm ashamed to be seen with them, if anyone from Glasnevin saw me, I'd die.

The lights come back up.

LINDA. I've had enough of this. Come on, girls, we're going…

GER. Like hell you are, Linda! I'm warning you…

LINDA. 'I'm warning you, I'm warning you.' Is that all you know how to say?

LISA. You're just making it worse, Linda.

JANET. Yeah, let's stay, I think they're gas craic!

LINDA. Are you joking, Janet! I'm not listening to any more of me ma's crap.

GER. I'm tellin' ya, if you walk out that door it'll be for the last time…

NEIGHBOUR (*off*). Will you stop screaming up there. We can't hear the telly.

ROSE goes out on the balcony.

ROSE. Ah get back in your box, ya louser!

NEIGHBOUR (*off*). I wasn't talking to you, Rose O'Brien!

ROSE. Oh yeah?!

GABBY. Rose, would you get back in here!

DOLLY (*referring to the neighbour*). Don't pay any attention to her, Mister Flanagan.

NEIGHBOUR (*off*). If yous don't shut up I'm going to call the Guards!

ROSE. Go ahead, we could do with some men up here.

GER. Rose, will you get back inside.

LINDA goes out the door with JANET and LISA.

She's gone! The little bitch. Walked right out the door. Can you believe it. I'm telling you she has me heart scalded with her 'office job' and her 'emancipation'. I feel like I need to break something. I really feel like I need to break something!

ROSE. Is she still into that Women's Lib? That's dangerous that is, Ger, she'll get herself excommunicated.

GABBY. And she'll never get a fella.

ROSE. Oh she has a fellah but he's an eejit.

GABBY. He'd have to be an eejit if he lets her be a Women's Libber.

LILLY. Politics isn't for women.

MARIE. And sure those Women's Libbers are off looking for johnnies and everything up in Belfast. Father Scully says they're a disgrace. Father Scully says they're Godless.

TERESA. As bad as the Italians!

DOLLY. Who's Johnny?

YVONNE. It makes sense all the same doesn't it? Contraception?

GABBY. Jesus!

ROSE. Wash your mouth out, Yvonne Long!

MARIE. I'm not staying here with heathens, Ger, what if Father Scully got wind of this conversation? I love my kids, every last one of them. I'd take six more if it was God's will. I'm surprised at you sayin' such a thing, Yvonne Long.

YVONNE. I just think...

GABBY. Well, don't think, Yvonne Long. You absolutely shouldn't be thinkin'...

ROSE. Coz that's dangerous.

Didn't the bishops warn us about 'thinkin''!

YVONNE. Not everyone wants to have a large family...

ROSE. Shhhhh, would ya... Jesus Christ, sure they'd all be at it night and day if they thought they wouldn't get pregnant... the whole of Dublin would be one big...

DOLLY. Orgy!

She says it and then goes scarlet.

ROSE. Exactly, Dolly.

MARIE. This has to stop. This talk has to stop right now or...

GER. Yes, stop it, stop it please. In my house. Dear God, help us, I'm mortified. You see what she started, Rose…you see what my Linda started…

ROSE. You'll have to rein her in, Ger…

TERESA. Yes you'll have to rein Linda right in, Ger, or there'll be trouble…

LINDA (*off*). Sorry, ladies.

ANGELA (*off*). Linda Lawless, how are you? Is your mother inside?

RUTHIE (*off*). We didn't miss the party did we?

ROSE. Here come Ruthie and Angela, Ger, you better get a grip on yourself.

LINDA (*off*). No… they're all in there…

RUTHIE (*off*). And where are you off to?

LINDA (*off*). We're just going out.

ANGELA (*off*). Ah come in and tell us your news, we haven't seen you in ages and we brought cake. There was loads of cake at the funeral…

LINDA (*off*). No thanks, Angela, we were just…

JANET. Ah come on, Linda. Let's have a slice of cake. I'm starvin'.

LISA. And it's freezing out there.

RUTHIE. It's a black-forest…

JANET. I love a black-forest.

LINDA, JANET *and* LISA *enter with* ANGELA SMITH *and* RUTHIE BARRETT.

GER. Is that you, Angela?

ANGELA. Yes it is. Oh look at everyone…

RUTHIE. What a crowd! God save us is there room for us at all?

THE OTHERS. Hello, hello. Come on in, how have you been?… (*Etc.*)

RUTHIE. Sorry I'm a bit out of breath. We had to walk up all them stairs, Mrs Lawless.

ANGELA. The lift was broke again...

ROSE. Not to worry, Ger will surely be getting a new one with her stamps!

They all laugh except RUTHIE *and* ANGELA *who don't understand.*

GER. Very funny. Very funny, Rose... Linda, will you go get two more chairs for the ladies.

LINDA. Where? There aren't any more chairs...

GER. So go in next door and borrow a few poufs or something!

LINDA (*to the* GIRLS). Okay... okay... come on, girls...

GER. And don't think you're off the hook, young Linda Lawless!

They leave, LISA *and* JANET *grab some cake on the way.*

DOLLY. Here, take my seat, Ruthie...

TERESA. Yes, come and sit next to me, Angela.

ANGELA *and* RUTHIE. Thank you. Thank you very much.

RUTHIE. That's an awful lot of stamps you've got there.

GER. Yes, a million!

ANGELA. Oh my God...

ROSE. So she's glad of the extra hands.

MARIE. And we know you Maggies aren't shy of a bit of work.

ROSE. Marie! Jesus...

GABBY. They don't like people knowing their business...

MARIE. I'm sorry, I didn't mean anything...

ROSE. Sure me tongue is paralysed from lickin', Ruthie.

RUTHIE. You've been doing it with your tongue?

GABBY. Of course not, she's just being funny...

ANGELA. Well, we're very happy to give you a hand.

ROSE. So long as you don't give us some tongue…

She laughs awkwardly. No one laughs.

GER. So, how was the funeral, girls?

Blackout. Spotlight on ANGELA *and* RUTHIE.

RUTHIE. Oh it was a good funeral wasn't it, Angela.

ANGELA. It was. Though the flowers were a little lacklustre…

RUTHIE. Did ya think?

ANGELA. I did and the prayers of the faithful?

RUTHIE. Yes, a bit rushed.

ANGELA. Maybe it was on account of him going so quick?

RUTHIE. True, I never thought he'd go before us, sure we've known him since he was knee-high and now he's gone and we're still here.

Shockin'.

ANGELA. Shockin'.

RUTHIE. We'll not last long now, Angela. Sure there's nothing left of me.

Seventeen operations and two stints in Peamount.

ANGELA. One stint in Peamount.

RUTHIE. A lung, a kidney, two gallstones, an appendix and one of my breasts…!

ANGELA. Poor Ruthie. And I'm crippled with the arthritis.

RUTHIE. Poor Angie.

ANGELA. And poor Rory Fagan.

RUTHIE. God rest him, Rory Fagan and he only forty. Forty is too young to die…

ANGELA. Josie told me how it happened.

RUTHIE. Did she? Was it bloody?

ANGELA. No.

RUTHIE (*disappointed*). Ahhh.

ANGELA. He got home from work, Rory Fagan, last Monday
night, and Josie thought he looked a bit strange.

RUTHIE. Pasty?

ANGELA. Pale as a ghost.

RUTHIE. White as a sheet.

ANGELA. So she said, 'Are you feeling all right, Rory?'

RUTHIE. And he said...?

ANGELA. 'Shut up, the lot of you'...

RUTHIE *jumps*.

...to the childer because they were making a racket.

RUTHIE. Isn't that terrible.

ANGELA. Desperate! And then the daughter...

RUTHIE. Clara...

ANGELA. Clara. Well, she started giggling at something so he
stretched over to give her a belt and didn't he suck in his
breath and keel over into his stew!

RUTHIE. No!

ANGELA. And that was the end of him!

RUTHIE. All over.

ANGELA. All over.

RUTHIE. Desperate.

ANGELA. It was that sudden, I'll tell you, Ruthie. We should
be all down on our knees...

RUTHIE. Praying for a peaceful death.

ANGELA. The Lord said it. I'll come like a thief.

RUTHIE. Like a thief in the night.

ANGELA. You never know the day nor the hour...

Make sure I get confession in the morning.

RUTHIE. I will of course, after Francie Moriarty's funeral.

ANGELA. Francie! Is that tomorrow?

RUTHIE. It is.

ANGELA. I hope they do a better job on the sandwiches.

RUTHIE. I'm sure they will, Mary Moriarty works at the Kylemore.

ANGELA. Oh isn't that nice. Just make sure I get my confession.

RUTHIE. Don't be worrying, Angela, you're going straight to heaven I'm sure of it.

ANGELA. No it's you that's going straight to heaven, Ruthie.

RUTHIE. Not like Fagan's daughter. Did you see the look on her face at the funeral?!

ANGELA. She's in a desperate state. Thinks she killed the father.

RUTHIE. Good enough for her. It's a sin to be giving cheek to your father.

ANGELA. She better make her confession.

RUTHIE. God is good.

ANGELA. Isn't that the truth and I thought he looked well all the same, in the coffin, didn't he? Mr Fagan. Almost like he was smiling.

RUTHIE. He's gone to his reward, Angela, it's the living now deserve our prayers.

And did you notice that the sister didn't show up?

ANGELA. Fagan's sister?

RUTHIE. No, Josie's sister.

Divorced.

ANGELA. Dear God... No!

RUTHIE. Married an American and got a divorce.

ANGELA. Them Americans are mad for divorce!

RUTHIE. Mad for it.

ANGELA. You'd never get that here...

RUTHIE. No, no wife-swapping sodomites in Ireland.

ANGELA. Thank God.

RUTHIE. She's got a boyfriend and all now for herself!

ANGELA. She hasn't?

RUTHIE. She has. Such a disgrace. A disgrace to the whole
family.

No more than Patsy Guerin.

ANGELA. Shhh don't let Ger Lawless hear you. You know she
gets very upset about her sister.

RUTHIE. I'm not surprised. A tramp if ever I saw one.

ANGELA. I always thought Patsy was nice.

Spotlight on GER.

GER. Patsy. Me sister Patsy. She was the pet of the house. She
was the baby and we all doted on her, it's true but she... she
ran off, she... we don't speak now. She ran off with a gurrier,
a gurrier-born, didn't even finish her schoolin' and broke me
mother's heart. And she was always the favourite, Patsy,
everyone's favourite, spoilt rotten, maybe that's what
happened to her. 'Hand me down a star,' that's what Ma used
to say because Daddy would have climbed the sky and got a
star for Patsy, if Patsy would have wanted one. He loved her,
she was the baby of the house and nothing was too good for
her and then she went and ran off...

ROSE. And we weren't even jealous of her, Patsy. None of us.
Coz we all loved her. She was like a doll, a real live doll and
we used to dress her up coz we had a few bob spare at that
stage with me married and the others finished school and Ger
workin' before she got married so we'd buy all sorts of little
outfits for Patsy. I remember Mammy even bought her a coat
in Clerys. Clerys! Raspberry-red it was, with little wooden
buttons. She was like a little princess in it. Like in the photos
you'd see of the Royals. And she was quick, Patsy. Top of
the class at everything in school. The nuns loved her. Had
their eye on her to be a nun or a teacher with her prizes for

English stories and prizes for religion, yeah, can you believe it? Prizes for religion. Her favourite book was the *Lives of the Saints*, she knew the story of every one of them and her favourite was 'The Little Flower', Saint Teresa of Lisieux, she used to wear a little Saint Teresa medal, I think I still have it somewhere. Da never got over it when she ran off... it was like a huge hole... a huge hole in our house and our lives and when I think of her now, well... I wonder is she all right... I wonder is she lonely?

GABBY. She tried to bring him home once but there was hell to pay. Da said he was a bad 'un from the start and Patsy was supposed to be studyin' anyway, Patsy was doing her leaving cert and the nuns said she could do well and be a teacher, that was always the plan. She had brains to burn, Patsy, but then she went and fell in with Charlie.

THE THREE SISTERS. Goddamn Charlie! He was a bastard out of hell. It's all his fault. He led our Patsy all astray and broke our father's heart, broke our mother's heart. Goddamn that bastard. Goddamn that Charlie.

RUTHIE. I don't know what you mean 'nice', Angela. Patsy Guerin works the streets.

ANGELA. I don't think so, Ruthie.

OLIVE *starts singing her 'Dicey Reilly' song again.*

TERESA. For God's sake.

The lights come back up: TERESA *gives* OLIVE *another smack on the head.*

GER. Beat the brains out of her if you have to, Teresa. She's giving me a headache.

TERESA. I'm not about to kill her just to make you happy.

ROSE. You might as well, she'd be better off dead the way you treat her.

TERESA. What? What did you just say?

ROSE. Nothing.

MARIE. It's you pair that is giving me the headache, you never stop fighting, Rose.

ANGELA. Has there been a fight?

RUTHIE. We should have come sooner.

TERESA. I won't listen to your insults, Rose O'Brien...

LILLY. And they're off.

ROSE. Just put the poor woman out of her misery instead of dragging her through the flats trying to look the martyr.

GER. Rose, for God's sake.

TERESA. I'll never forgive you for that, Rose O'Brien, never.

ROSE. Ah, get lost, I'm sick of listenin' to ya.

RUTHIE. Who started it?

ROSE. What does it matter who started it?!

ANGELA. We were only asking...

ROSE. Why? So you can blab it all over Balbutcher is it?

RUTHIE. Please don't start shouting at Angela.

ROSE. I'll shout at who I want to shout at!

MARIE (*to herself*). I'll just grab another one of them books.

GABBY (*who has seen her*). What are you up to, Marie?

ROSE. I should have stayed at home, honest to Jesus, me nerves are gone with this crowd.

MARIE. Shhhh! Just take these and keep quiet!

ROSE. I'm not able for it...

> LINDA, JANET and LISA *arrive with the chairs. There is a great hullabaloo. All the* WOMEN *change places, taking advantage of the occasion to steal more stamps.*

DOLLY. Don't overdo it there, Marie, she'll notice!

TERESA. No she won't, sure she's got a million, here stick a few books under Mother!

The door opens suddenly and PATSY GUERIN *comes in.*

PATSY. Where's the party?

THE OTHERS. Patsy! Patsy Guerin!

ANGELA. Oh my God!

GER. What are you doing here? I hope nobody saw you coming into the flats?

PATSY. I heard about your big win so I thought I'd come over and share in the celebrations.

Angela! Angie, is that you? What are you doing here?

Everyone looks at ANGELA.

Blackout.

Interval.

ACT TWO

The second act begins with PATSY*'s entrance. Hence the last six lines of Act One are repeated now. The door opens suddenly and* PATSY GUERIN *comes in.*

PATSY. Where's the party?

THE OTHERS. Patsy Guerin!

ANGELA. Oh my God!

GER. What are you doing here? I hope nobody saw you coming into the flats?

PATSY. I heard about your big win so I thought I'd come over and share in the celebrations.

Angela! Angie, is that you? What are you doing here?

Everyone looks at ANGELA.

ANGELA. Oh my God! I'm found out!

GER. What do you mean, 'found out'?

PATSY. Angie and I are friends aren't we, Angie?

ANGELA. I'm afraid I don't feel well.

ANGELA *pretends to faint.*

RUTHIE. Jesus, what's happened to her?

GABBY. Is she dead?

RUTHIE. What?

ROSE. Don't be daft, Gabby, I think she fainted.

PATSY. And I think she's only pretending.

PATSY *approaches* ANGELA.

GER. Don't touch her, you!

PATSY. I told you she's a friend…

RUTHIE. That is a scandalous accusation!

GER. Angela Smith is a respectable woman, she is no friend of yours.

PATSY. Really? How come I see her down Leeson Street then, almost every Friday night.

ALL THE WOMEN. Leeson Street!

RUTHIE. That is impossible.

PATSY. Ask her yourself. Why don't you stop playing dead, Angie, and tell them, you won't go to hell you know, Joys is only a nightclub.

ANGELA (*after a silence*). All right, it's true.

Now RUTHIE *keels over!*

GABBY. So is she dead now?

SOME OF THE WOMEN. Joys! That's a disgrace.

SOME OTHER WOMEN. Joys! That's abominable.

LINDA, JANET *and* LISA. Joys! Her! You're having us on.

The lights go out. RUTHIE *lifts her head up.*

RUTHIE. Angela! Angela!

Spotlight on ANGELA *and* RUTHIE.

ANGELA. Please, Ruthie, let me explain.

RUTHIE. It's not true. It can't be true!

THE WOMEN. Isn't it always the quiet ones!

RUTHIE. Leeson Street! It's a den of iniquity, Angie, what on earth were you doing there?

ANGELA. I just go to socialise…

RUTHIE. SOCIALISE!

THE WOMEN. Always too sweet to be wholesome!

GER. God only knows what goes on in them basements!

ROSE. Is she trying to get a fella at her age!

ANGELA. No, No, honestly, I don't do anything wrong!

PATSY. It's true. She doesn't do anything wrong.

YVONNE. Is it some kind of service perhaps? For the prostitutes. Like a soup run?

PATSY *laughs*.

ROSE, GER *and* GABBY. It's not soup they need, Mrs Long, it's lockin' up!

RUTHIE. I have never felt so betrayed.

ANGELA. But I just like to dance.

ROSE, GER *and* GABBY. Dance?!

ROSE. I'll tell you I've heard it all now.

ALL THE WOMEN (*except the girls*). Depraved! Depraved it is. Dancing is depraved. Sure didn't the bishops warn us! Dancing is dangerous. A mortal sin. A mortler. You'll be dancing your way to hell because dancing will be the ruin of you like it's the ruin of all men. Swaggering and swinging and hips and lips and hell. It's the road to perdition. A road only for whores.

ROSE, GER *and* GABBY. Like Patsy Guerin.

ALL THE WOMEN (*except the girls*). Shame on you, Angela Smith, what would the nuns say that reared you?

PATSY. Would you get a grip of yourselves. She only comes to dance.

ROSE, GER *and* GABBY. See! You see! The bishops are always right. You're a danger, Patsy Guerin, with your loose ways and your liberation, you have her dancing with the devil.

LINDA, JANET *and* LISA. The devil? For God's sake, would you listen to yourselves. Stuck in your flats morning, noon and night, peering through the curtains and shakin' at the thought of the world! There's nothing wrong with nightclubs, there's nothing wrong with dancing. You're living in last century.

THE WOMEN. Ah yeah it's easy to laugh when you're young. It's easy to mock. But mark my words, them places are full of temptation. Them places are full of vice. If you lose yourself in gyrating. You might lose yourself entire. And then it's too late. Too late.

LISA. Too late! It's too late! Oh my God, it's too late!

GER. You'll have to get down on your knees, Angela Smith.

ROSE. And to think that every Sunday I see you at Communion... with a secret like that in your heart.

ANGELA. Ruthie, please. You're my best friend in the whole world, you're like a sister to me, you know that, you're all I've got. We've been together since we were babies. Worked the laundry, minded the new babies, prayed, cleaned the little oratory, cleaned the church, always did what we were told, never snuck out, never went with boys, stayed true to Christ we did, stayed true to the nuns and then got our little flat. And I was so happy, we were so happy. We have our grand jobs and go to the funerals and you have your choir on a Friday and that's... that's when. It was just something different where I can be someone different but I don't do anything wrong. I just dance and I meet people and I laugh, really laugh, laugh like I've never laughed in my life.

RUTHIE. Laughter is a sin!

PATSY. No it's not, it's good for you.

RUTHIE. You have to swear you'll never go back.

ANGELA. But I like it...

RUTHIE. If you don't turn your back on Patsy Guerin. If you don't turn your back on... I can't even bring myself to say it. Then I'll turn you out, Angela. I mean it. I'll not be associated with Leeson Street! Dear God in Heaven, what will people think? What will people say? I don't know what's come over you, Angela, you'll have to go the priest, you'll have to go back to the nuns. But if you go back to one of those clubs then I'll never ever speak to you again.

ANGELA. Ruthie, please...

RUTHIE. No! Not a word until you promise.

The lights come up. ANGELA *sits in a corner.* PATSY *joins her.*

ANGELA. Why did you have to open your big mouth?

PATSY. Relax. They just love a bit of drama…

ANGELA. It's easy for you, Patsy.

PATSY. No, you're wrong there, Angela. Nothing is easy for me.

ANGELA. Ruthie means what she says. She'll never forgive me now. I'll be ostracised like you. Sure Lilly's on the Catholic Action Network, now she'll be on to Father Scully and he'll be on to Father Flanagan and they'll get on to Sister Bernadette. And I'll be a pariah, I'll be ruined, Patsy, just like you.

GER. Patsy!

PATSY. I only came over to stick in some stamps, Ger, and to see you, to see my sisters and my niece. There is nothing wrong in that.

ROSE. You should have thought of that years ago, when you walked out!

GABBY. You cause nothing but trouble, Patsy Guerin. Nothing.

ANGELA. Please don't break up the evening. I'll go.

LILLY. I think you should both go.

ANGELA *gets up.*

ANGELA (*to* RUTHIE). Are you coming home, Ruthie?

RUTHIE *doesn't answer.*

I'll leave the key under the mat so.

She goes towards the door. The lights go out. Spotlight on ANGELA.

It's easy to judge isn't it. It's always easy to judge. Ireland is awash with it, Dublin is drowning in it, the flats are on fire with it and we all squirm and scream in silence under the curse. I've been judged all of my life. That's what happens when you grow up in the convent, when you're born into it. Fallen. I fell into this world a fallen woman, a fallen child. I've never known my mother and I've never known anything different than to judge or be judged. Ruthie's the same, but she doesn't see it. Ruthie's plan was to be good, always good and

to tell when the others weren't. We never got out you see. No
one adopted us. No nice lady came and took us away like the
other children, the other babies. On account of me being plain
I suppose and Ruthie's club foot. So we worked our way out
through the nursery, the dormitory, the laundry, the front hall,
the kitchens, the infirmary, the office and the gardens, and we
stayed good, always good. We prayed, we were good little
Catholics and we kept our heads down. So eventually the
priest found us two jobs as housekeepers and the corporation
gave us a flat and we were free. It might have taken forty years
but Ruthie's plan got us free. Freedom can be lonely but.
Freedom can be hard. It took us a long time to manage the
shopping and the bills and the opening your own front door.
And seven years ago when we all moved into Ballymun and
Patsy came round with a gift for one of Rose's babies, there
was hell to pay and Rose threw her out of the child's
christening. She did! She threw her out in front of everyone
and I could hear all the commotion up the stairwell… sure
you'd have heard it out in Drimnagh. And then I could hear
Patsy coming down the stairs and I could hear her stifling back
the sobs and I felt right sorry for her I did. And then she
sat down on the last step to try and sort herself out a bit
I suppose… and I looked out the door and she saw me and
I asked her would she like a tissue and she said she would and
then she said she'd love a cup of tea and I felt so sorry for her
with her beautiful curly hair and her lovely shoes and all… and
the gift still under her arm. Well, I thought she looked like an
angel there, a kind of a broken angel and her lip all curled up
and a drop of blood on it. I wouldn't be surprised if Rose had
swung at her… so… I brought her inside, sure what else could
I do and then she sat down on my chair, Patsy, and I washed
her face for her and she was lovely and kind and it made me
think of our Lord and Mary Magdalen and we had a chat and
she was grand she was by the time she was leaving. Patsy
never judged, she was happy in her own life and she wasn't
afraid. That's what marked her out. So I was delighted when
I met her again after all this time and she remembered me, and
she invited me down to where she worked. It was a Friday and
Ruthie was at her choir. I'm barred coz I can't sing and I put
the others off so I went down with Patsy to Leeson Street and

it was such an eye-opener, another world. Joys isn't the young club where Patsy started, it's for the older crowd and although it's full of loneliness, there's a comfort in it because it's dark and we can pretend. We can pretend the cheap wine is mother's milk and we can pretend that we belong. That we are real people with real worth and real lives. We can dance there in the darkness and pretend that we are young. That we are free. That we are loved. I never had a chance to pretend when I was a child. The real world never forgave me for being born. The real world never let me forget that I was a sinner. Now I'll have to stop going down. I'll have to stop pretending and live with who I am.

She goes off. Lights out. Spotlight on YVONNE.

YVONNE. Last week, my sister-in-law, Florence had a birthday. They had a really nice party for her. There were gangs of us. First there was Florence and her family. Oscar Darcy her husband, Florence Darcy, that's her, and their seven kids: John, Kathleen, Louie, Teresa, Mary, Jane and Hugh. Her husband's parents, Franklin Darcy and his wife, Betty Darcy, were there too. Next, there was my sister-in-law's mother, Mary Doyle. Her father wasn't there because he's dead… Then there were the other guests: Vinny Finnegan, his wife Linda, Ronan Keenaghan, Hughie Keenaghan, also, Willy Gott, Jane Fagan, Peter Leonard and his wife, Nessa D'Orcy, Des, Alan, Lorraine O'Farrell, Caitriona Lonnergan, Napoleon Byrne, Sabrina O'Toole, Nathan Harrington, Ruth O'Sullivan, Brian O'Sullivan, Grainne Kinsella, Nónín Keagan, Siobhra Naughton, Karen Louw, Kevin Dean, Gráinne Doyle, Maveve Wright, Alexander Towhee, Aidan Green, Seanie Maxwell and his wife Sadhbh, Maureen Collender, Gerry Kelly, Denise Byrne, Sara Barry, Sandra Byrne, Tony Noctor, Gary O'Farrell, Finbarr Sweeney, Joe Byrne, Patricia Carroll, Nora Carroll, Betty Carroll, Joan McAuliff, Sean Carroll, Mary Carroll, Gerald Carroll, James Moran, Molly Blackburn, Janie Grace, Deirdre Moynihan and us, my husband, Barny, and me. I think that's just about everyone…

The lights come back up.

GER. Okay, girls, we better get back to these stamps or we'll never finish them.

ROSE. On your toes, girls!

DOLLY. We're not doing too bad, are we, Ger? Look at all the ones I've pasted...

MARIE. What about all the ones you've stolen...?

LILLY. Do you want to give me some more stamps, Mrs Lawless?

GER. Good girl, Lilly, here's another batch.

RUTHIE. I'm not sure that I'm going to be much good to you, Mrs Lawless, I'm that shook with Angie and everything... .

LINDA (*to* PATSY). I hate the way they talk to you, Auntie Patsy, I'm really sorry.

PATSY. You've nothing to be sorry about, Linda.

LINDA. But it's mortifying and Ma's only getting worse. She never listens. She never changes. I'll tell you, me and Robert are saving every penny we have and we're getting the boat to London. Out of this kip.

GER. I hear there's a trip to Knock coming up after Easter.

ROSE. Father Scully announced it last Sunday.

MARIE. I hope it won't be the same price as last year, that was prohibitive that was.

GABBY. And it's hard to be asking mothers to stay overnight, who'll be cooking the dinners at home?

YVONNE. Not Father Scully in anyway!

ROSE. I like it when we get to stay overnight!

LILLY. I believe Father Flanagan is going to take the group this year.

DOLLY. Oh yeah? He's good lookin' he is, Father Flanagan.

GABBY. And young...

LILLY. And his sermons are to die for.

ROSE (*to* GABBY). There she goes again with her Father Flanagan. We'll be hearing about him now for the rest of the evening. I think she has a glad-eye for him!

GABBY. He's a bit too modern for me. Starting that folk group and the sports days for the kids an' all.

ROSE. I agree entirely, Gabby. I'm sick of hearing about him. And that sports day he organised is mixed, did you know that. I don't think that's a good idea sure didn't the bishops warn us about that. Mixed athletics is dangerous in them shorts... just the top of a slippery slope.

LILLY. The man is a saint... and very charismatic. When he speaks, Mrs Doyle, it's almost like listening to Jesus himself.

TERESA. Don't be losing the run of yourself there, Lilly.

LILLY. But don't you see how the children just adore him.

She starts to sing 'Suffer little children and come on to me'.

ROSE. What's that noise?

GABBY *laughs*.

LILLY. Father Flanagan will be singing that with the Communion class as part of the Parish Charity Night. They have been practising for months.

DOLLY. What's on the programme?

LILLY. There's going to be all sorts, Dolly and Mrs Grady's little boy is going to sing 'Kyrie Eleison'!

ROSE. Well, that's something to look forward to. Maybe he'll crack a few windows. I'm sick to death of that kid, his mother's been unbearable since he got a solo on *Prayers on One*.

LILLY. He has a beautiful voice, Mrs O'Brien.

ROSE. Shame about the face.

GABBY. Rose!

LILLY. Deirdre Dolan will be dong a reading from the Old Testament.

ROSE. That's sure to pack them in, Lilly.

Any door prizes?

LILLY. Definitely, and the concert will be followed by a giant bingo!

THE OTHER WOMEN (*except the* GIRLS). A bingo!

Blackout.

When the lights come back up, the WOMEN *are all at the edge of the stage.*

While ROSE, GER, GABBY, TERESA *and* MARIE *recite the 'Ode to Bingo', the four other* WOMEN *call out bingo numbers in counterpoint.*

ROSE, GER, GABBY, TERESA *and* MARIE. Is there anything in the world like bingo?! Once a month there's a bingo in the Parish Hall and the whole of Ballymun is quakin' with anticipation. Me, I get ready two days in advance. I have me bingo pens and me readin' glasses and spare pants just in case it gets too thrilling. I'm all wound up, I can't sit still, and me head is full of two-fat-ladies, legs-eleven, two-little-ducks and the doctor's-orders. And when the big day arrives, I'm up the walls! I can barely get the batch under the grill. The house goes to the dogs so it does and the minute they finish their tea, I'm in the bedroom gettin' changed. I put on the bit of lipstick, me new nylons and pull the hair well out of me eyes. Wild horses couldn't hold me back when I hear all the doors openin' at the one time, and all the steps on the stairs and all the coats swishin' and the chat and the clatter and the rush of feet as we march out from Pearse, Plunkett, McDonagh, McDermott, Clarke, Ceannt and Connolly! A legion of us. An army of us, cross the court and head into the hall. I love playing bingo! I just fucking love playing bingo! There's nothing in the world can beat bingo! And when we get there, the hall is full of smoke and there's a run for the lucky tables and a scramble for the chairs and bingo pens and handbags and headscarves all go flying, till everyone's got their spot, got their cards, got their specs and are all set. All set for the BINGO.

The game begins!

The WOMEN *who are calling out the numbers continue alone for a moment.*

It's all I can do to stay sittin' in me chair. Me heart is pumping. Me fingers are flyin'. Me ears are sticking up like that radio mast in Donnybrook. I can't breathe. I can't stick it. I get all mixed up. I'm sweating like a pig. I screw up the numbers. I can see the cow to me right is only waiting for one! Me nerves is gone. I've put me 'X' in the wrong squares. I get the caller to repeat the last number. I think I'm going to faint because I love playing bingo! I fucking love playing bingo! There's just nothing in the world can beat bingo! Now the night's nearly over and I haven't won a shaggin' thing but I've got three more goes. Two down and one across. All I'm missing is the B14! I need the B14! I want the B14! I look at the auld-one next to me. Shit, she's as close as I am. Can I stab her with me pen? Can I blind her with me cap? Can I strangle her with me scarf because I've got to win! I've got to win! I've got to win!

LILLY. B14!

THE OTHERS. Bingo! Bingo! Holy Jesus, it's bingo!

And what I have won?

LILLY. Two bookends in the shape of Chinese dogs!

THE OTHERS. Two bookends in the shape of Chinese dogs! Just what I've always wanted! I love playing bingo! I fucking love playing bingo! There's nothing in the world beats bingo! It gives meaning to my life. It makes me a person. It makes me a winner. I only wish they'd let us play it once a week. Long live bookends. Long live Chinese dogs. Long live bingo!

Lights to normal.

ROSE. I'm parched, any chance of a little lubrication there, Geraldine?

GER. Oh yes of course, I got a few bottles of fizzy. Linda, will you serve out the Cokes.

OLIVE. Parched. I'm parched.

TERESA. We'll get you a glass of something, Mother, but I forgot your sippy cup so don't go spilling it all over yourself.

ROSE. Do you hear her! Do you hear her, Gabby?

GABBY. I'm sitting right beside her, Rose.

GER. Don't start again, Rose, just concentrate on your stickin'.

ROSE. It's not a sweatshop you're running ya know!

Spotlight on the refrigerator. The following scene takes place by the refrigerator door.

LISA (*to* LINDA). I need to talk to you, Linda.

LINDA. I know, you said so down The Penter, what is it?

LISA. I've got to tell someone or I think I'll burst. I just can't hide it much longer. I can't hold it much longer. You're me best friend, Linda, I need you to... I need... I need...

LINDA. Jesus what is it, Lisa?

LISA. I'm pregnant.

LINDA. What! You're joking... No? Are you absolutely sure?

LISA. Yes, I'm sure. I went to the doctor and all I did.

LINDA. Which doctor?

LISA. Not Cronin, I went to one in town.

LINDA. Jesus! What are you going to do?

LISA. I don't know. Well, I do know. I don't want to know. I can't tell me ma, it'll kill her, Linda and I'm sure me da will kill me. I'll tell you, I feel like jumping off a fucking balcony.

PATSY. Don't do that, Lisa. Don't even think of it...

LINDA. You heard her, Auntie Pats?

LISA. Don't tell anyone, Patsy, please...

PATSY. I won't. Of course I won't. I can help you, Lisa, it's not the end of the world. You know there's a way out.

LISA. I know, but who? Where? How?

PATSY. Women take the boat every day.

LISA. Do I have to go to England?

PATSY. I wouldn't trust the backstreet doctors here.

LINDA. Patsy, Jesus, she can't do what I think you're talking about...

PATSY. So what would you suggest, Linda? Do you think this lot will come round if she has that baby? Do you think they'll all start knittin' her little booties and help her pick out a nice new cot? You know what happens when a young-one round here comes home pregnant.

LINDA. But what you're talkin' about is killin'. What you're talkin' about is murder!

LISA. I told you, Linda. I'll kill meself if I have to go through with it. I've thought about it already, but I don't know where to go. There must be someone here, Patsy, I've never been out of Dublin...

PATSY. It's safer in England, Lisa. Much safer than here. You'll go to a proper hospital. I can help you arrange it if you like. A week from now it could be all over.

LINDA. *Lisa*, you can't do it, you just can't do it!

LISA. What would you do, Linda? Look at Mary Blake, for fuck's sake. Stuck in the flats for the rest of her life, livin' with her ma and a da that won't so much as look at her. All the lads say she's a slut, even the bastard got her pregnant in the first place. She can't cross the court without someone shoutin' abuse at her and the baby. The auld-ones will have nothin' to do with her. She'll never get a job. She's finished she is. Finished... before she even started.

LINDA. But what about the father? Who is the bloody father? Is it Joe? Why don't you just get married?

LISA. No it's not Joe. It's someone else.

LINDA. WHO?

LISA. I met him in town. He works in town. He works in an office and he promised me the moon, he did. Used to bring me off in his car. Touring up the mountains and then we'd stop for our lunch in this nice little old hotel. Money was never a problem and he was always talking politics and askin' me my opinion. Who ever asks you your opinion around here, on anything except their fucking hair? And he made me feel like someone. He bought me new shoes and he bought me this chain and I thought everything was roses because I'm a fucking fool I am and now I think the bastard's married. He's gone anyway. Gone runnin' as soon as I told him and do you know I don't even have his phone number. We used to meet up at Parnell Square, under that statue you know of the Swans coz he used to talk about statues and buildin's and history and I lapped it all up didn't I? Like the gobshite that I am. Now he's gone. Gone in his fancy car and I don't know where to find him. And I want that life, Linda. I want to know what's goin' on in the world. I want to talk about buildin's and I want to get a good job and have good clothes and real bracelets, not the plastic shit you get on Talbot Street. I want a proper life, not stuck workin' in the chipper shovelling up greasy fish to drunks till two in the morning. I want more. I want to make something of meself, that's why I'm doing that commercial course. That's why I paid for it meself. I'm getting' out of here, Linda, and I'm going to be somebody.

LINDA. Well, you're not off to a great start!

LISA. Don't be a bitch, please. I've no one and I need to fix this.

PATSY. We understand, don't we, Linda. Sure you want to get the hell out of Dublin yourself. I know what it feels like, girls. I remember it well. Them walls in the flats are like prison walls aren't they. There's no room for a little ambition is there? That's too threatenin' altogether. Father Scully and your da and the lads on the corners, they just want to keep you right where you are. You better not show that you've got brains and you better not show that you've got ideas... then you're done for. And your ma won't protect you will she, coz she's too busy having more babies and cookin' more dinners. She can't see beyond the walls. I didn't start workin' in the chipper, girls, I went straight to where the money is, and me and Charlie, we're flying down on Leeson Street and I'm only one step from a life of real money and real adventure...

ROSE, GER *and* GABBY. Goddamn Charlie! Goddamn Charlie!

JANET. What are yiz whispering about over there?

LISA. Nothin'. (*To* PATSY.) Thanks, Patsy, you're a life-saver… can we talk again about all this later?

JANET. Talk about what?

LISA. Forget it, Janet, it's nothing!

JANET. I thought you told me everything?

LISA. Will you drop it, Janet… please!

GER. What's happening with them Cokes, Linda?

LINDA. Coming, coming…

The lights come back up.

GABBY. I thought you'd wear your new blue suit tonight, Rose, how much did you say you paid for it?

ROSE. Six pound it was. I'm keeping it for good wear.

GABBY. I saw it in Arnotts for twelve.

ROSE. Did ya? Fair play to Francie Toner so, he said I was gettin' it cheap.

GABBY. That Francie Toner must have lifted it!

ROSE. Nothin' to do with me. I paid me six pound fair and square I did.

LILLY. My Mary just got a new job in Plunkett Designs actually, and they deliver to Arnotts. She says they have fabulous new machines now for dyeing all the fabrics…

MARIE. I heard them machines are fierce noisy but. Me sister-in-law's daughter had to get her ears tested after workin' on them… she had a ringing in her ears for weeks. I was only talking to her mother about it on the phone earlier…

ROSE. Oh my God, I forgot, Linda, you're wanted on the phone!

LINDA *runs to the phone.*

LINDA. Hello? Robert? Jesus! How long have you been waitin'?

JANET. Tell me what's going on, Lisa?

LISA. I can't, Janet, I just can't. I need to talk to Patsy.

JANET. Okay, I get the message! You and Linda are always in cahoots about something...

LINDA. I didn't know you were waitin, Robert. She didn't tell me. Yeah, I know, it's not my fault. Do you think I want to be stuck in here...

TERESA. Now, Mother, stop shifting yourself, I just need to put these in your pockets.

ROSE. So how are things with you, Janet love? How is UCD!!??

JANET. Oh, it's grand, it's great so it is.

ROSE. And how does your mother afford all them books?

JANET. I get a grant.

ROSE. What's that?

GABBY. It's free money, Rose, from the corporation.

ROSE. Well, isn't it well for some. I don't know how you stick all that book-reading all the same. I can't imagine it's good for you.

JANET. It's hard to get the time I need to study at home. I have to stay late in the library most nights.

ROSE. Most nights, really!... slippery slope...

GABBY. So who helps your mammy with the dinner and gettin' the little ones to bed then?

JANET. I don't know. I think Mark does when he gets in from his football.

GABBY. Your brother! Holy God, I wouldn't have that. That's not natural is it, Rose.

ROSE. Certainly not, you can't have your brother helpin' with the dinner.

JANET. Da does it too sometimes.

ROSE. Did you hear that, Gabby... even the father cooks! That won't end well...

JANET. I do me bit, Rose. I do all the washin' for Mam at the weekend and I get everyone out to school before I get me own bus but still I get nothing but hassle from Mark, from Da, from everyone…

LINDA (*on the phone*). Oh, do what you want, Robert. I'm tellin' you it's not my fault! Ring me later when you're finished huffin'.

She hangs up.

For God's sake, Auntie Rose, why didn't you tell me Robert was on the phone? He's after eatin' the face off me!

ROSE. I must say you're polite now you are, Linda! Lovely and polite.

Spotlight on PATSY.

PATSY. When I left me ma's house I was in love. Starry-eyed and so bloody stupid. No one else in the world existed, only Charlie. He soon turned me away from me ma, me friends, me sisters. He knew what he was doing. I could have been anything I wanted to be. I had the looks and the brains. He told me he was going to make me a model. I could see myself in one of them perfume ads. I could see myself in London, New York, Paris. I was a fool, always lookin' to tomorrow, always lookin' to Charlie. Now I've wasted thirteen years of my life on Leeson Street. Leeson Street! Calling men into the club, holding out the wine menu, tempting them inside. I was his poster girl, he'd no intention of letting me go to London, New York, Paris. And I made him a fortune I did… crossing the floor in my killer heels, sitting on laps, being groped, tipped, mauled. And he took it all. Every penny! He kept me sweet with titbits all right, a bit of glitter, promises and magazines. When I think of it now I rarely saw daylight for the first few years. Leeson Street was my life, and now I'm old. Thirty is too old in this game. I don't even do the door now on his hip new place, he has me stuck in Joys. He'll have me cleaning the toilets next. I'm fucked. I could jump off a balcony myself coz I'm not like Lisa, she thinks she's finished just coz she's pregnant but that can be looked after, there's no doctor can fix me, no doctor can give me back those years. What have I got now? What the hell am I going to do now? I have to stop the drinking and think. I don't know where to go. I don't have anywhere to go. Can I really try me sisters? Might they hand

me down a star? No, not a chance... look at them... crushed
they are... crushing... Jesus, what am I going to do now?

LISA. What am I going to do now? I never wanted this. I was
careful. Just that one time. That one time and now, Jesus,
the thoughts of going to England. Will I be all on my own?
I don't even have a passport. I wonder does that matter.
I can't let this stop me. Won't let this stop me. I want me ma
to be proud of me... and me da. I can't ever... ever let them
know. I wish I was like Patsy. She doesn't care about
anyone. She's got it made. She doesn't care what her sisters
think of her, what anyone thinks of her, she's got her Charlie
and she runs her own life.

PATSY. He threw me out on the street. Like a dog on the corner
of Rathmines Road. I think he has already moved the new one
into our flat, the new me. Poor fool, doesn't know what she's
letting herself in for. I've nothing to me name now bar the
clothes on me back. What's left for me now but Fitzwilliam
Square? God no, the thoughts of it. Standing in the shadows.
Hoping. Waiting. Praying that you turn a trick so you can get
in out of the cold. I've seen the faces of the women down
there. Broken, bruised, battered faces tangled through the ivy,
clinging to the corners, generations of them, like ghosts...
You age fast down there on the square... you're lucky to get
out with your life... but what choice do I have? I'll have to do
it for a few weeks... take me chances... get some cash... and
hold on to it and start again. That's the only way out coz
I won't get a job around here... what was I thinkin? Sure they
barely let me in the door tonight and if I try get a job like
Lisa... in the chipper or in the shop, then they'll all know that
Charlie's dumped me and they'll all know that I was duped.
No. I'll just have to put a brave face on it... a new face on it,
I'll have a drink I will, I'll have a drink and find a way.

LISA (*interspersed throughout* PATSY'*s last speech*). I'm so
frightened. Dear God, please, I'm not bad, not a bad person,
I just, I just can't have this baby. I hope you understand,
I didn't mean it, I'm not able, please, please look after me,
I'm not... and I'm so, so scared!

She approaches PATSY.

Are you sure I'll be all right, Patsy? Are you sure they'll take me in a hospital over there?

PATSY (*laughing*). Of course you will. You'll be grand, Linda. You just need money.

LISA. Money?

PATSY. Yeah...

LISA. Where do I get money?

PATSY *shrugs*.

The lights come back up.

MARIE. It's not even safe for a girl to go to the pictures these days. I went to *The Towering Inferno* at the Carlton last Tuesday. I was supposed to be going with me sister but she had cramps and cancelled so I went in anyway coz it's so rare that I get a night out. Well, all of a sudden, doesn't this smelly auld letch in a trench coat sit down beside me and he starts sliding his hand over my knee so he does. Well, it took me a minute to realise that it wasn't an accident and I nearly died so I did. I stood up, there and then, took a swing of me handbag and smashed him right in his ugly mug so I did!

DOLLY. Good for you, Marie! I always carry a knitting needle with me when I go to the pictures. You never know what might happen. And the first fella that puts his hand on my knee will get it in the eye!

ROSE. Holy God, but you're a terror, Dolly Snow! You'll empty out the Carlton so you will!

Ger, these Cokes are a bit flat.

GER. When are you going to stop criticising me, Rose? Tell me when?

LISA. Linda, have you got something I can write on? I want to get Patsy's number.

LINDA. Going to England is not a good idea, Lisa, anything could happen you and... and, are you not afraid about God?

LISA. God hasn't come up with any other options, Linda, so I've no choice! I'm telling you I am not going to have this baby. I've made up my mind. The only question is how.

RUTHIE (*to* TERESA). What are you doing with them books, Teresa?

TERESA. Shh would ya. She has plenty... she'll never notice.

RUTHIE. But that's stealing...

TERESA. No it's not, she didn't pay for them did she?

RUTHIE. I don't think that's fair, Teresa.

GER (*to* ROSE). What are those two talking about? I don't like whispering...

She goes over to RUTHIE *and* TERESA.

TERESA (*seeing her coming*). Oh... Yeah... Well, you just add two cups of water and stir.

RUTHIE. What? (*Noticing* GER.) Oh! Yes! Teresa was just giving me a recipe.

GER. A recipe for what?

RUTHIE. Fairy cakes!

TERESA. Chocolate pudding!

GER. Well, which is it? Fairy cakes or chocolate pudding?

She comes back to ROSE.

There's something fishy going on here, I know by them....

ROSE (*who has just hidden a few books in her purse*). Don't be daft, Ger, you're just exhausted, you're imagining things.

GER. And you're spending too much time up there with Patsy, come over here, Linda, where I can keep an eye on you.

LINDA. In a minute, Ma, we're just talking.

GER. That's what I'm afraid of! Come on over here I said I want ya!

LINDA. Okay! Okay.

GABBY. What are yiz talking about anyway?

GER. Yeah, what's going on with Lisa, she doesn't look herself at all this weather?

LINDA. Nothing, Ma...

GER. What kind of nothing?

ROSE. I saw her writing something down a minute ago?

LINDA. It was just Patsy's number.

GER. What does she want with Patsy's number? Are you two planning on goin' over to her place? I've warned you, Linda, you're to have nothing to do with her...

LINDA. Jesus, Ma, will you lay off! You're such a drama queen.

GER. I'm warning ya...

LINDA. Yeah, yeah I heard.

She goes back over to PATSY *and* LISA.

ROSE. God, she's getting terrible cheeky, Ger.

GER. I know. I told you, she has my heart scalded.

ROSE. Reminds me of Patsy when she was home.

GER. That's all I need. I'll tell you this is the one and only time Patsy Guerin gets into this flat, and if she starts hanging around my Linda, I'll throw her down the bloody stairwell I will.

MARIE. Did you see that Tracy Martin on the sixth floor. She's getting' very heavy isn't she?

LILLY. Yes, I've noticed her at mass...

TERESA (*insinuating*). Strange, isn't it? It's all in her middle.

ROSE. I hope she's not in some kind of trouble!

MARIE. She won't hide it for much longer.

TERESA. I wonder who got at her.

LILLY. It's probably the stepfather...

GER. I wouldn't be surprised, he's a letch, don't know what Betsy Martin was doin' letting him next nor near the place.

TERESA. Sure what choice did she have? Seven kids and no wages comin' in the door but he's notorious all right... always chasing the young ones.

ROSE. I don't know, that Tracy Martin is a bit of a rip if you ask me. Stepfather or no stepfather, did you see the length of her school skirt?! I mean what mother would let her child go around like that. And last summer, in the heatwave, did you see them red shorts she had! Red! Shorts! I mean what do you expect and then she's always flicking her hair, flickin' it this way and flickin' it that and the length of it. It's not natural. And the waddle on her. I'm tellin' ya, I said it to meself last summer that one will turn out bad and wasn't I right? They've no one but themselves to blame these young ones. Oversexed is what they are.

GER. Rose!

ROSE. I've no sympathy. They're only askin' for it.

LISA *starts to get up*.

PATSY. Don't be listening to her, love.

ROSE. Flauntin' theirselves in shorts and mini-skirts. It's an epidemic is what it is and Father Scully agrees with me, it's all these Women's Libbers and too much telly and not enough religion! Down on their knees is where them young-ones should be, not trotting around getting buses and lookin' for office jobs! Who do they think they are? Now I know there's some of them gets raped and that's different, so long as they're in their own homes when they're attacked and not out lookin' for it. Because the young ones walkin' around Ballymun and gettin' theirselves up the duff, well, they get no sympathy from me. If my Carmel ever came home pregnant, I'm telling you, I'd put her through the window I would! Not that I'm worried mind. She is a good girl, Carmel. Knows how to keep her knickers on and that's all it takes, a bit of respect, a bit of dignity. Sluts is all they are. Sluts and cockteasers is what most of them are, that's what my Dessie says, and he's right.

LISA. Stupid bitch.

JANET. What did you say? I think Rose is right.

LISA. For God's sake, Janet...

PATSY. Isn't that a bit much, Rose?

ROSE. Ah well, Patsy Guerin, what more can we expect from you? Sure you've no morals, no, you threw them out years ago when you went off with that Latcheco, Charlie. Haven't even had the decency to get married. That is if he'll even marry you at this stage. Well, there's no one interested in free love here thank you very much, we're all good Catholics and know what free love leads to!

PATSY (*laughing*). Haven't you ever heard of the pill, Rose?

ROSE. The pill doesn't save you from eternal flames, Patsy. The pill is only for whores.

YVONNE. I think that might be a bit strong, Rose. There are times when a young girl might find herself in trouble and it's not entirely her fault.

ROSE. You! You're just watching too many of them plays.

YVONNE. Plays!

ROSE. Everyone knows the sort that goes in for plays – dangerous! Free-thinkers! And it's the same with the films because films try to make you feel sorry for people. They try and make you see things different. Well, I've no interest in seeing things different. I know my catechism and I know a slut when I see one. Real life isn't like the films and real life isn't like a play, when a young one here comes home pregnant, she's only got herself to blame. Full bloody stop.

LISA. What does she know, the ignorant auld bitch and the way she talks about her daughter Carmel. Imagine having a mother like that and Carmel O'Brien is no angel neither. I've a good mind to tell the old bag.

Spotlight on ROSE.

ROSE. That's right. Life is life and no movie-man or no play-writer ever made anything about that.

Of course an actress can make you feel sorry for her in a film with the big doe eyes and roughed-up shoulders. Sure that's dead easy that is. And then I bet she heads home to some big mansion with a big bedroom and huge bed with fancy sheets and fancy carpet and some handsome hunk has left her diamonds and chocolate. But what about the rest of us? What do we get? Grabbin' hands. That's all that's ever waitin' for me in my scabby-arsed bed. Gruntin' and squeezin' and always at me, morning, noon and night with his droopy eyes and his drippin' nose and his stubble scrapin' the face off me. Every morning without fail he has a yen on him. I can't lie peaceful once the sun rises coz he's up and risin' with it! He's like a vulture he is. Pickin' over me carcass. Turnin' me and twistin' me so he can get himself his favorite angle. You don't see that in the films do ya! You don't see that on the bleedin' stage! They don't write women like me. They don't write real women who have to lie on their backs to please selfish pigs just coz they made a mistake and once said yes to him! No fucking film was ever that sad because no film or no play lasts a lifetime. THIS lasts a lifetime though, THIS. Why... why oh why did I ever let him near me. I should have said more than no. I should have yelled no, no, no, no, NO at the top of my lungs and stayed single. At least I'd have had some peace! But I was such an innocent in them days, I didn't know what he was at or what it all meant or how you got yourself pregnant. And then, it was too late. There was nothing for it but to marry the bastard. I blame my mother. She told us nothing. All I knew is that it was a sin to be with a fella but sure everything's a bloody sin in Ireland, from riding bikes to wearing bras. You'd never be up to them bishops. They would simply have ya standin' in your kitchen all day long, sayin' nothing, thinkin' nothing, just cookin', cookin' and liftin' your arse up good and regular for your husband. And spittin' out babies. Oh yes, you've got to spit out them good little Catholic babies. Once a year and no messin'. They'd cut you in two for them good little Catholic babies. Well, my Carmel won't get caught, I can tell you that. Because I've warned her I have. I've been warnin' her since she could walk that men are to be feared and men are bastards and you've got to put a lock on your nether regions coz they only want one thing and that's to poke at you and tear you right open. It made her kind of timid, I'll admit as a child. Terrified like. Collapsing if ever she seen a man that wasn't her brother or her father. But isn't she better off! She won't be tellin' me I didn't warn her! And she won't end up like me will she? She won't end up at forty-four with a rake of snotty kids from teen to toddler and another one in the oven.

She won't end up with a randy slob of a husband who's as thick as the wall and demandin' his conjugals every day of the week. I'll tell ya, when you get to this age and know that you've nothing behind you and less ahead of you, it'd make you want to run. Run and run and run but women can't do that can they? Not real women. Not Irish women. No. They get caught by the throat real early and then they stay quiet don't they, they stay quiet, lyin' on their back right to the end.

The lights come back up.

GABBY. I like the odd foreign film I do.

GER. Where would you see a foreign film?

GABBY. America is foreign isn't it? I like them cowboy films. And them cowboys are real good looking, real tough, real men they are.

GER. They're no better lookin' than Irish men.

Everyone laughs.

MARIE. Who'd put an Irish fella in a film?

ROSE. With the cabbage-head on him!

MARIE. Lumping about the place…

GABBY. Though that Father Sheehy in *The Riordans* is a bit of all right.

MARIE. He's a priest, Gabby!

GABBY. Not in real life he isn't.

ROSE. He's no John Wayne though is he…

MARIE. Or Steve McQueen.

GABBY. Oh Jesus… Steve McQueen!

ROSE. Queenie I O, who has the ball, is he big or is he small!!!

Everyone laughs again.

OLIVE. Coke… Coke… More… Coke…

ROSE. Give her a Coke and shut her up will you, Ger.

GER. I think I've run out.

ROSE. Of course you have.

Talk about cheap.

RUTHIE (*as she steals some stamps*). Just two books and I could get a nice chrome dustpan.

ANGELA *comes in.*

ANGELA. Can I come in?

No one answers, just look to each other.

I went to see Father Scully, Ruthie. Got him up from his tea I did and I got my confession.

PATSY. For God's sake, don't let them bully you, Angela.

ANGELA. No I'm not listening to you, Patsy, you're a bad influence that's what Father Scully said.

GER. Are you listening to that, Linda!

DOLLY. You were right to go to the priest, Mrs Smith. Jesus will never see you stuck.

GER. How many books have we filled now do ya think?

The WOMEN *sit up in their chairs.* GABBY *hesitates, then speaks.*

GABBY. I meant to tell ya, Ger, I found this fabalas dressmaker and she still makes corsets. I know you were lookin' for one for that yellow-print dress for the trip to Knock.

RUTHIE. I knew you'd come to your senses, Angela. We'll both go to early mass for a week to make amends.

LISA. Jesus, there's no hope is there, Patsy?

PATSY. All she ever did was dance.

LINDA. It's suffocating it is, and they're all the same, all...

PATSY. Broken.

LISA. That's why I'm gettin' out. We've got to get out, Linda, or you'll end up just like your ma, thinking a non-stick frying pan makes you a person.

LINDA. I know, she's fucking tragic isn't she!

GER. Gabby, that's marvellous, I'd almost given up hope. It's impossible to get a good corset...

She goes over to the box that is supposed to hold the completed books. The WOMEN *follow her with their eyes.*

Mother of God, where are all me booklets? There's no more than a dozen in that box?

Silence. GER *looks at all the* WOMEN.

Hey! What's goin' on here?

THE OTHERS. Well... Ah... What do ya mean... They must be here somewhere...

They pretend to search for the books. GER *stations herself in front of the door.*

GER. Where's me stamps?

ROSE. I don't know, Ger. Sure amn't I killed lookin' for them!

GER. They're not in the box and they're not on the table! Where's me bleedin' STAMPS!

OLIVE (*pulling stamps out from under her clothes*). Stamps? Stamps... Stamps...

She laughs.

TERESA. Mother! What are you doing? Mother!

MARIE. Jesus Mary and all the Saints!

DOLLY. Pray for us!

GER. Her clothes are full of stamps! What the fuck... she's got sheets of them in every pocket... and under her arse and all! Teresa Doyle... have you... have you been robbin' my stamps?

TERESA. How dare you!

GER. Let me see your bag!

TERESA. I have never in my life!

ROSE. Ger, don't be ridiculous don't you know they're here somewhere!

GER. You too, Rose. Show us your handbag! I want to see your handbag, every one of yiz!

DOLLY. That's a shockin' accusation, Ger!

YVONNE. Shockin'!

LILLY. I'll never set foot in this flat again!

GER grabs TERESA's bag and opens it. She pulls out several books.

GER. Would ya lookit! Lookit! All me stamps and I bet you're all the same. Every last one of yiz.

PATSY. Were they knockin' them off! Can you believe it! The sanctimonious bitches.

GER. Show me your bag, Rose!

ROSE. No!

She grabs ROSE's bag.

GER. Jesus Christ, it's full to the brim.

She grabs another purse.

And you too, Yvonne, and you too, Dolly Snow.

ANGELA. And Ruthie!!!!

GER. Robbers. Robbers. Every one of yous is a bleedin' robber!

MARIE. You never should have got them in the first place.

DOLLY. You're not even nice!

ROSE. And you made us all feel like shit with your fluorescent plastic tins and synthetic shag!

GER. But they're mine, Rose. Them stamps are mine!

LILLY. A true Christian would have shared them. Given everyone a share!

THE OTHERS. Yeah, everyone a share!

GER. Give them back! Give them back this instant!

THE OTHERS. No! Not a chance! Get off!

MARIE. There's a lot more in the boxes. I'm helping meself.

DOLLY. Good idea.

YVONNE. It's only just!

GER. Stop it! Stop it! Keep your hands off them!

TERESA. Here, Mother, take your share.

MARIE. There's tons of them here!

PATSY. Leave them in the box, Marie Doyle!

GER. Me stamps! Me stamps!

ROSE. Give us a hand here, Gabby!

GER. No! No! Me stamps!

A huge battle ensues. The WOMEN *steal all the stamps they can.* PATSY *and* GER *try to stop them.* LINDA *and* LISA *and* JANET *stay seated in the corner watching with their mouths open.*

Screams are heard as some of the WOMEN *begin fighting.*

MARIE. Give me that bunch, they're mine!

ROSE. You're a lyin' bitch, Marie, they're mine!

LILLY (*to* GABBY). Let go of me! Let me go!

They start throwing stamps and books at one another. Everybody grabs all they can get their hands on, throwing stamps everywhere, out the door, even out the window. OLIVE *starts cruising around in her wheelchair singing the Irish National Anthem. A few* WOMEN *go out with their loot of stamps.*

ROSE *and* GABBY *stay a bit longer than the others.*

GER. Me sisters! Me own family stealin' from me. I can't believe it!

GABBY and ROSE *run out. The only ones left in the kitchen are* GER, LINDA *and* PATSY. GER *collapses into a chair.*

All me stamps! Me stamps!

PATSY *puts her arms around* GER's *shoulders.*

PATSY. Don't cry, for God's sake…

GER. Don't talk to me you…

PATSY. But I didn't take any, Ger.

GER. Get out, just get out, Patsy, I don't want you here…

PATSY. But I tried to help. I'm on your side.

GER. No you're not. You're just scum, Patsy Guerin. Scum worse than the rest of them.

PATSY turns to leave. She looks to LINDA.

PATSY. You were right, Linda. Hopeless.

LINDA. Ma…

GER. And don't talk to me you either. Don't talk to me…

LINDA (*sighs*). You haven't a clue have ya, Ma?

You're fucking blind aren't ya… blind to everything…

GER. No I'm not, Linda. I'm not blind and I'm not stupid… So go on, go on with the others. Go on to The Penter or to town or wherever it is you're going and leave me be will ya, just leave me in peace.

LINDA *hovers, then leaves.*

Because it's too late isn't it, it's too late for me, it's not too late for you…

Too late.

And there's nothing. Nothing left now. Me stamps. Me beautiful stamps. Me beautiful new home! Me new life, it's gone isn't it? It's all gone. I've got nothing.

She falls to her knees beside the chair, picking up the remaining stamps. She is crying. We hear all the others outside softly singing the Irish National Anthem.

As the song continues, GER *regains her courage.*

Ah fuck it. Fuck the lot of ya.

She finishes the song with the others.

A rain of stamps falls slowly from the ceiling.

End.

www.nickhernbooks.co.uk

facebook.com/nickhernbooks

twitter.com/nickhernbooks